Soft Scien

Soft Science Sustainability

Educating for Otherwise Futures

RAGNHILD UTHEIM

About the front cover: Bøyabreen glacier is an arm of Jostedalsbreen (Jostedal glacier) easily accessible from the main road in Fjærland, between Oslo and Florø—Norway's westernmost town. Growing up, we passed by this glacier in the summertime on our way to my father's childhood home in Sunnfjord. Jostedalsbreen is the largest glacier in continental Europe, with more than twenty arms that reach out into valleys below, but is retreating fast. The sketch below is traced from photographs and reveals its retreat from 1997 to 2019. Photo by Ragnhild Utheim.

Bøyabreen glacier in 1997 (left) and in 2019 (right).

For information, contact State University of New York Press, Albany, NY
www.sunypress.edu

Library of Congress Cataloging-in-Publication Data

Name: Utheim, Ragnhild, author.
Title: Soft science sustainability : educating for otherwise futures / Ragnhild Utheim.
Description: Albany : State University of New York Press, [2024]. | Includes
    bibliographical references and index.
Identifiers: LCCN 2023029855 | ISBN 9781438496948 (hardcover : alk. paper) |
    ISBN 9781438496962 (ebook) | ISBN 9781438496955 (pbk. : alk. paper)
Subjects: LCSH: Interdisciplinary approach in education. | Environmental
    education. | Sustainability. | Climate justice.
Classification: LCC LB1027 .U76 2024 | DDC 375—dc23/eng/20230809
LC record available at https://lccn.loc.gov/2023029855

10 9 8 7 6 5 4 3 2 1

Contents

Illustrations

Acknowledgments

I would like to acknowledge and extend my thanks to those who reviewed my manuscript and to SUNY Press for helping me through the publication process. I am particularly indebted to Jesse Goldstein, whose thoughtful and thorough feedback proved incredibly meaningful and allowed me to rethink aspects of the manuscript.

I further extend my thanks and appreciation to those who have, more generally, helped me find my place in academics over the years. My gratitude goes to my cherished anthropology colleagues at Purchase College for always supporting me: Rudi Gaudio, Jason Pine, David Kim, Lorraine Plourde, and Shaka McGlotten. My gratitude also extends to colleagues in my unit who I have learned to know better in recent years and who make Purchase College such a special place to work: Megan Rossman, Melissa Forstrom, Laura Ricciardi, Maria Guralnik, Janis Astor del Valle, Dawn Gibson-Brehon, Jordan Shue, Mara Horowitz, Ursula Heinrich, George Keteku, Leandro Benmergui, Matthew Immergut, Els van den Bosch, and Stella Kristensen.

I am beyond grateful and honored to work alongside an incredibly inspiring and dynamic group of professionals in my role as director—thank you Rudi Gaudio, Aviva Taubenfeld, Paula Halperin, Chris Robbins, Jack Tamburri, Jenny Undercofler, Nelly van Bommel, and Casey Hooper for making the difficult years since COVID-19 more manageable, and for encouraging moments of laughter through it all. There are many more colleagues I could mention that I am so grateful to know and be able to work with as part of our college community. It is a common refrain to hear that what people love most about Purchase College is their colleagues and students. Nothing echoes more clearly how I feel, especially during a time when uncertainty and change looms large across higher education.

My thanks also go to colleagues, students, and friends at the Bedford Hills College Program, where I taught for many years. I have learned more from my students at Bedford Hills than I could ever teach anyone. A special thanks to Michelle Ronda, who has been an amazing research partner and friend through the years.

In particular, my gratitude goes to Lisa Jean Moore and C. Ray Borck for helping me stay grounded and maintain perspective, and supporting me with this project. Finally, I am forever grateful for my dear friends, near and far, and my family: my beautiful children, Tor Håkon and Kaya; my partner in life, Rogerio; and my loving parents, Oddrun and Bjørnar Utheim.

Introduction

The World Is Our Neighborhood

Where are we going? . . . and why am I in a handbasket?

—Bumper sticker

In hospital-speak, Code Red alerts fire and initiates the R.A.C.E. response: Rescue those in danger; Activate the fire alarm; Contain the fire; and Extinguish the fire. It was the acronym used by the Intergovernmental Panel on Climate Change (IPCC) to sound the sirens in their sixth climate change assessment report (2021): "code red for humanity." The earth is our home and the world our neighborhood, but if we take the symbolism to its logical conclusion, we may be ablaze in fire far sooner than anticipated. Global climate champion Greta Thunberg, famed for being a "kind but poorly informed teenager" (President Vladimir Putin) and needing to "work on her anger management problem" (President Donald Trump)—among more notable things—was eloquently indignant when addressing leaders at the Austrian World Summit on climate change in 2021:

> More and more people around the world have woken up to the climate and ecological crisis, putting more and more pressure on you, the people in power. Eventually, the public pressure was too much and you had the world's eyes on you. So you started to act. Not acting as in taking climate action, but action as in role playing, playing politics, playing with words and playing with our future, pretending to take responsibility, acting as saviors as you try to convince us that things are being taken

1

care of. Meanwhile, the gap between your rhetoric and reality keeps growing wider and wider, and since the level of awareness is so low, you almost get away with it. But let's be clear: What you are doing is not about climate action or responding to an emergency. It never was. This is communication tactics dressed as politics, disguised as politics. You, especially leaders from high income nations, are pretending to change and listen to the young people while you continue pretty much exactly like before.

For all her might and conviction in rousing world leaders from their theatrics and slumber, I am reminded of a colleague's indisputable aside: Greta Thunberg cannot solve the climate crisis alone.

Our need to invest in a common language with global reach as climate change advances and the environmental challenges confronting planet earth intensify is now more urgent than ever. Despite the scientific warnings and political commitments from nations worldwide, greenhouse gases have continued to rise (United Nations Environment Programme, 2019). In their *Emissions Gap Report 2019*, the United Nations Environment Programme (UNEP) revealed bleak findings—with improvements well below what scientists had targeted and hoped for—and emphasized the "need for rapid and transformational action" (p. iv).[1] The UN 2030 Sustainable Development Goals (SDGs) have emerged as a framework around which a common language and related civic discourse can materialize. Bundled into seventeen composite goals that target critical areas of need, the SDGs and their multicolor wheel logo have become a symbol of our need to unite globally around environmental destruction, climate change, and species extinction caused by human activity. Achieving the 2030 SDGs will require concerted commitments that span sectors of local society worldwide, however, including civil society, business, government, international bodies and organizations, media, and education.

The central role of education in particular, in responding to the clarion call of mobilizing around sustainable development, is noted among stakeholders across the international arena. In its *Issues and Trends in Education for Sustainable Development* report, UNESCO[2] singles out education as "one of the most important drivers of change" in response to the challenges before us (Leicht et al., 2018, p. 29). Yet for education to live up to its potential and alter the current trajectory of global climate change, it must be "flexible, culturally sensitive, relevant and suited to changing people's values and behaviors" (World We Want, 2013, iv). As the UNESCO report concludes, education itself must change, to become more holistic, critically reflexive, and transformative, if it is to act as a vehicle for sustaining earth (p. 29). This book examines what this need for change within education might look like, narrowing in on a series of core competencies that have emerged as part of curricula that engage sustainability as a foremost issue of our time.

Because drivers of climate change involve multidimensional, intersecting processes that are both global and local in scope, educating to sustain the future will require more than tinkering at the edges and will remain ineffectual without integrating expertise that spans society, science and its disciplines, cultures, and histories. Curricula will need to uncover how global systems and structures with adverse consequences for the environment interconnect and adapt in dynamic ways across space and time (Papenfuss et al., 2019). In other words, efforts to discern anthropogenic drivers in diverse world localities will require collaborative responses that combine interdisciplinary knowledge, multicultural understanding, and world historical analyses (Fiske et al., 2018; Rosa & Dietz, 2012). Despite the need for investment from all fronts, the social sciences and humanities have been comparatively underrepresented in efforts to advance knowledge of the factors involved, however, while Eurocentric perspectives continue to dominate education content.

Sustainable development is often conceptualized in terms of the scientific fields of study that make up the *three Es* of sustainability: ecology, economy, and (social) equity. A general consensus has emerged within the field of education for sustainable development (ESD), however, regarding the centrality of certain "core competencies" upon which sustainability education must additionally build—above and beyond the scientific knowledge needed. Included are such metacognitive skills as systems-thinking competency, anticipatory competency, normative competency, strategic competency, collaborative competency, critical-thinking competency, self-awareness competency, and integrated problem-solving competency (Osman et al., 2017).[3] This book is intended as a point of departure for envisioning and distilling the soft science competencies that environmental challenges necessitate, but that exist beyond the realm of scientific discovery and invention, the competencies needed to critically reflect and collectively act on and synthesize complex (and often conflicting) knowledge in response to the challenges before us. Said simply, it will take more than STEM and hard sciences (as significant as these are) to solve the problems before us.

Education for sustaining our common future must necessarily draw from diverse worldviews and build on curricula from across designated fields of study, theoretical perspectives, and pedagogical frameworks in responding to shifting demographics, technologies, and world geopolitics in increasingly turbulent and polarized times. The field of competing expertise, authorities, and pedagogies on best practices for educating students about our "common and uncommon" historical present and how to move toward a more sustainable future is vast and crowded, however (Stein, 2018a). Following in the footsteps of scholars who use cognitive mapping and social cartography as a collaborative research tool for outlining "relations between and within various epistemic communities and discursive and interpretive frameworks" (Suša & de Oliveira Andreotti, 2019, p. x), I weave together and critically engage work underway in multiple fields as part of evolving discourse on sustainability education, including education for sustainable development (ESD), environmental justice (EJ), critical theory (CT), global citizenship education (GCE), alternative development, critical and inclusive education (CIE), culturally responsive education (CRE), critical pedagogy, systems thinking theory, post-normal science, and more.

Organized around a social cartography of sustainability competencies, the book explores metacognitive and socially embodied, subjective intangibles at the crossroads of science and this assemblage of knowledge fields. Introduced in chapter 1, the *3C cartography* includes three broad categories—*contemplative criticality, compassionate collaboration,* and *comprehensive complexity*—and comprises a living, social cartography of expansive sustainability competencies across three spheres that encircle the 3E model and its curricular content (see figure 1.2). The ingredient competencies of the 3C cartography are intended as a dynamic and evolving inventory of component parts that intersect and intersperse, their frame of reference adjusting according to diverse sociocultural and historical particulars that inevitably influence perception. Conceived as a means to visualize, integrate, experiment with, and imagine the possibilities for (alternate) sustainable futures, the proceeding chapters examine this living inventory of sustainability competencies.

Interspersed throughout the book are also anecdotes, personal experiences, and testimonies that bring life to the teaching-learning nexus of academics, to static text or imagery on a page. This necessarily reflects my own journey of discovery and understanding, and efforts to learn from and share with others—students, colleagues, friends, family, or even people I may not know—ways of thinking about and engaging with the world. Many of the largest lessons in life materialize through exposure to unfamiliar cultural context, when the comfort of predictability is desta- bilized and our expectations are derailed. This may include immersion into transnational or diasporic cultures that span the physical globe, or intercultural encounters that emerge from social segmentation closer to home (i.e., class, regional tradition, religion, etc.). For me, many such lessons have transpired while teaching inside a maximum security prison for women in the United States, amid the morass and violence of mass incarceration. What it means to be discriminated against, dispossessed, exploited, alienated, dehumanized, and vulnerable takes on drastic dimen- sions inside the carceral spaces that configure human captivity.

It is behind the concrete walls and barbed wire of prison that some of the most palpable examples of soft science sustainability became apparent to me, long before the seventeen global goals were clearly articulated. The strengths of the UN global goals are at once their weakness: the enormous ambition and unwieldy reach for all-encompassing inclusivity overwhelms. Yet their import is precisely the sweep with which they legitimize nested, interconnected dimensions of what it means to sustain fulfilling life on earth. Many of the SDG targets contained in this "shared blueprint for peace and prosperity" justify the need to address inequality, deprivation, and social malfunctioning; many of these same targets are conspicuously wanting inside facilities where humans live out long sentences, year after year. As Dostoevsky noted long ago, "the degree of civilization in a society can be judged by entering its prisons." As microcosms that speak truth to power, the voices of those inside prisons magnify erudite perspectives vanished from the public view.

As someone who was not born and raised in the United States, teaching a study abroad course in my country of origin (Norway) during the summer of 2022 provided another unusual opportunity to learn from my students by defamiliarizing the familiar. Although naive distinctions between native and nonnative have long since lost their luster in a glo- balized world (Narayan, 1993), the cross-cultural experience of teaching foreign students in my country of origin allowed me to glean firsthand a host of reactions they had to local life in unfamiliar lands. Most striking was their relative awe and incredulity in response to the extensive public services that the Scandinavian welfare state provides (universal healthcare, tuition-free higher education, efficient public transportation, access to cultural institutions at subsidized or no cost, preservation of and proximity to nature). Their observations reinforced awareness of the destructive force that neoliberal restructuring has had over the last four decades in dispossessing people of basic public provisioning and a safety network.

In particular, students remarked on the overall sense of security and peace of mind they would enjoy had they been ensured the public services they witnessed during their visit. Not surprisingly, student debt was high on the list of grinding preoccupations. To what extent are you able to prioritize concern over climate change in the shadow of abject anxiety about sustaining your livelihood while repaying prohibitive student debt? The narrative culls from these and similar life experiences, memories, and musings thereupon for rhetorical purposes. Any anecdotal embellishments are, of course, evocative and purely illustrative; they are in no way intended as a form of fact-finding or truth-telling. Yet Archimedean scientific fact-finding in the abstract is a questionable form of truth-telling in its own right. What is the "true" meaning of facts devoid of human sentience and embodied experience after all? If we are to bring our infinite truths to the table, we need enhanced elasticity in our methods and approaches.

The culprit of climate change ultimately flows from one and the same source of domination over peoples and planet, a conviction explored throughout the book that I return to in its final pages. Education's mandate to adjust the destructive pathway we are on will be onerous worldwide. It involves radically rethinking human-centric assumptions prefaced on the separability of humans from each other and between humans and other-than-humans. Transforming the cultural values, social structures, economic arrangements, and relational configurations around which climate change converges entails teaching students to rethink how we think about institutions, systems, structures, processes, mechanisms, dynamics, meanings, purposes, approaches, methodologies, worldviews, cosmologies, ontologies, epistemologies, reasoning and rationality, histories and genealogies, time frames and temporality, space and place, and relations and interrelationships. This book and the 3C social cartography of soft science sustainability is an invitation to begin thinking, unthinking, and rethinking outside the confines of convention to unearth possibilities. As such, it is an invitation to add and accumulate missing pieces, remove parts that do not make sense, and adjust components that feel flawed or fail to suit circumstances.

Pathways for learning that interlink disciplinary subject matter and articulate connections between SDGs across fields of knowledge, in diverse global settings, will demand malleable pedagogical approaches and inclusive curricular content that enable students to explore "otherwise possibilities" together. It requires that we infuse metacognition with intentionality throughout education. Using sentient, collaborative models to guide learning toward this end, sustainability curricula must strive to integrate soft science sustainability competencies throughout formal education, with a focus on expanding the meanings and applicability of criticality and reflexivity; collaborating across disciplinary and cultural boundaries while connecting local and global knowledge; and acquiescing to a world reality in which dynamic change and knowledge uncertainty are the only constants.

Chapter One

Educating for Otherwise Futures

A recent interdisciplinary course on energy and society, offered at the public college where I teach, revealed that less than 50 percent of students attending the class (a total of 30) felt it was their responsibility to address climate change—this was entrusted to the next generation. As unscientific and decontextualized as this anecdote is, it proffers a stark reminder of our inadequate response to climate catastrophe. It takes a village to raise a child, but also a child to raise a village (Sen, n.d.). How do we empower youth to be(come) members of our global village, with the vision, agency, and resolve to build alternate sustainable futures? As noted in the introduction, climate change and sustainable development are commonly conceptualized in terms of the *three Es* of sustainability and their scientific fields of expertise: ecology, economy, and (social) equity. Yet it will take more than scientific expertise configured along the three Es to adequately address climate change. Before introducing the 3C cartography, I briefly outline the foundational pillars of sustainability featured in the classical 3E framework and contextualize the need for soft science competencies across intersecting knowledge domains.

Included as part of the 3Es of sustainability are the bounded disciplinary subjects that feed into and substantiate climate change, and inform the broad contours of sustainability expertise. Captured in the Venn diagram on the next page (figure 1.1), they are depicted as three overlapping spheres within which a series of complex and interrelated vectors of climate change intersect.

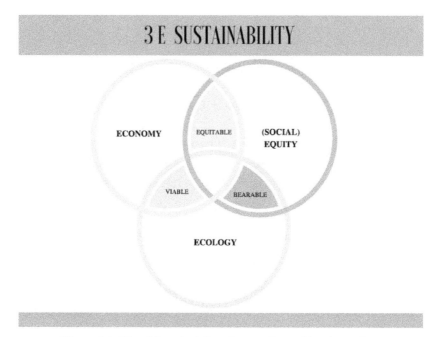

Figure 1.1. 3Es of Sustainability. *Source*: Created by the author.

The bottom 3E component as illustrated above is ecology and its carrying capacity. Broadly conceived in terms of the footprint of human activities, it includes variables like natural and cultural environment, resource consumption, material waste and waste management, energy production and expenditure, and so forth. The second E represents the economy and economic growth, which includes such variables as sustainable growth, efficiency and competitiveness, production and consumption, employment, and global trade. Because globalization has promoted uneven economic growth across world regions, a foremost challenge of this E implicates widespread economic inequalities. The final E includes equity—or social equity—and is sometimes referenced under the rubric 'society.' The (social) equity E addresses basic human needs related to essentials such as food and nutrition, housing, health, education, and so forth, which in turn correlate with human welfare, equal opportunity, and social cohesion.

As is readily inferred when analyzing the Venn diagram above, the indicators across the plane of the 3E model are far from exhaustive and are not mutually exclusive or restricted within any of their closed curves.

Each of the circles represent areas of overlap with other variables from across all three Es. In other words, we can assume that there are—to varying degrees, at any given time—intersections between the different vectors across all spheres. The 3E Venn diagram represents a mental map that renders more visible the complicated nature of climate change factors, as they adapt through space and time.

As a form of social cartography, visual maps like the Venn diagram provide a heuristic device for capturing the enormous complexity of sustainability, particularly when delineated to illuminate interconnecting forces at the granular level. The variables that impinge on our ability to move toward more sustainable lifeways are, more often than not, ambiguous and accompanied by infinite possibilities and a great deal of uncertainty. Moreover, although we may be able to conceptualize various indicators upon which sustainability hinges, they are often not easily quantified. This presents particular challenges in a world of science and knowledge accumulation that has, more and more, come to prioritize quantitative metrics as an overdetermined measure of validity.

Beyond the complexity, ambiguity, and immeasurability that environmental challenges forecast, there is a need to distinguish between sustainability competencies configured by subject expertise on the one hand and the "soft science" sustainability competencies configured by metacognitive faculties on the other (i.e., self-awareness, social and intercultural reflexivity, and collaborative aptitude). Put differently, within, between, and outside the domains circumscribing substantive knowledge, upon which the 3E model builds, we can identify a series of metacognitive knowledge competencies that transcend scientific bodies of expertise. They are often, although not always, implied rather than explicitly articulated. Representing requisite skill sets that are anchored in social and interpersonal relations, however, and that are fundamentally influenced by shifting dynamics of culture and circumstance, they remain all the more important to elucidate and cultivate in efforts to pave pathways toward more sustainable futures.

Metacognitive competencies implicate questions and processes for which objective, scientific, and measurable criteria are difficult to establish with exactitude: the possibilities for why people think, learn, and behave the way they do are infinite. This does not render the insight that reflexivity and introspection bring to light trivial, however. How do the rote lifestyle choices people make as part of everyday life across variegated landscape condition consumer patterns as a foremost anthropogenic driver of climate change, for instance? How do these differ across cultures and what forces and factors mediate their associated behaviors at the local level? How might we begin to envision, mediate, and move toward needed paradigm shifts in thinking that help us mitigate anthropogenic drivers contingent upon such lifestyle choices? What values, needs (perceived or real), and status concerns impact our ability to adjust behavior, in efforts to seek meaningful and fulfilling lives beyond consumer fetishism and fixation on things material?

The 3C cartography featured in the Venn diagram below (figure 1.2), depicts an expanding list of (soft science) sustainability competencies organized according to three broad categories: contemplative criticality, compassionate collaboration, and comprehensive complexity. As noted in the introduction, it is intended as a living, social cartography that maps emergent sustainability competencies across three spheres, encircling the 3E model and its curricular content.

As in the 3E model, the variables populating the 3Cs are considered neither discrete nor mutually exclusive. Building on an expansive volume of foundational resources already in circulation across areas of expertise, the 3C cartography endeavors to assemble and explore these core sustainability

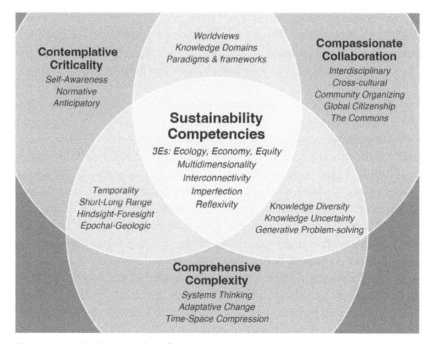

Figure 1.2. 3C Cartography of Sustainability Competencies. *Source:* Created by the author.

competencies. The competencies listed within and between each sphere of the 3Cs comprise an evolving, dynamic inventory of component parts that interact, their frame of reference adjusting across time and space (place). Each of the 3C categories can be thought of as three-dimensional and shifting—their ingredient parts integrating and intersecting, or dispersing and diversifying, in various directions and to varying degrees, intact (or not) with time.

Cognitive maps and mental mapping are useful for deciphering complex relationships and how intersecting phenomena configure lived experience and the world as we know it. They can assist us in navigating competing worldviews and knowledge claims that feed into collaborative problem-solving—despite seeming or presumed incompatibility—around the "wicked problems"[1] we face. As a participatory and iterative practice, social cartography challenges positivist notions of singular, objectivist knowledge, and attempts to disrupt universalizing claims implicit in dominant educational perspectives (Suša & de Oliveira Andreotti, 2019). Understood as a heuristic device in progress rather than prescriptive pro-totype, the provisional cartography explored in this book constitutes an animate and unfolding effort to explore, assemble, and experiment with multiple discursive perspectives and knowledge foundations, organized around core competencies that education will necessitate in addressing climate change and sustaining earth.

In visualizing a social cartography of sustainability competencies, the book entertains three overarching arguments. The first addresses the need to develop self-reflexive feedback mechanisms (checks and balances) across scope and scale (individual, collective, institutional, sociopolitical, geopolitical) that assist in identifying cyclical harmful processes (inequity, exploitation, oppression, domination), as part of knowledge accumulation and understanding that seeks to improve the human and other-than-human condition. This necessarily begins with individual biases and the arcane means by which they blind vision, but must map outward across the various communities to which we belong or do not belong. Sanitized corporate versions of implicit bias training are insufficient in redressing the specter of deeply buried biases. As Stein et al. (2020) argue, theories and enactment of change must employ pedagogies that anticipate modern colonial circularities grounded in skewed but comfortable visions of the familiar, while not "advocating any particular theory as 'the answer'" (p. 62).

The second, closely related argument invokes the need to develop mechanisms that assist us with "unforgetting" (Dunbar-Ortiz, 2008) and unlearning deeply ingrained ways of seeing, being, knowing, and relating that sustain domination, coloniality, and separability (across structures and systems, knowledge and understanding, relations and relationships, affect and habitus). This implicates the less comfortable encounters that visiting painful pasts involve—many of which live on in the present—and configuring ways to reconcile harm and pain. Feminist scholars have long been at the forefront of embracing and developing theory, pedagogy, and holistic mechanisms of learning that do not divorce knowledge accumulation from emotion and affect. Megan Boler's classic *Feeling Power* (1999), for example, examines the ways "emotions define how and what one chooses to see, and conversely, not to see" (p. 177). A pedagogy of discomfort must prepare for defense mechanisms, resistance to change based on conformity, and reactions to destabilized identities, when critical investigations challenge our values, beliefs, and self-image.

A final argument narrows in on our need to concede power and control to the complexity, ambiguity, and uncertainty that characterizes life and its pathways across human and nonhuman existence. This is not to resign hope, foresight, or the struggle for a common future, nor to disqualify the power of prediction, prescience, or hypothetical conjecture, but to heed the limits of control and disrupt our penchant to conquer the unknown (dominate) when control is beyond reach. It is to exercise humility in the face of forces that are larger than life. Students, teachers, and lifelong learners in search of what it means to live on and sustain earth in all its complexity—what it means to live *with* all life on earth—need to cultivate higher thresholds for uncertainty, unpredictability, and things unknown.

Unequivocal mastery of the unknown models (of learning) feed into the "instrumental framing of education as servant of a predictable future" (Amsler & Facer, 2017, p. 1) and contributes to the machinations by which the future/unknown is preemptively "captured," "foreclosed," and "colonized" (Amsler & Facer, 2017, p. 2). From early on, formal education habitually elicits "correct" answers from students who, in turn, learn to expect predictable and determinate solutions, as they move up the learning food chain. Students inculcated by subject specialization as the baseline of learning are de facto dissuaded from digressing curricular content or rummaging interrelationships. As a result, intentional metacognitive strategies and competencies that encourage us to appreciate complexity and adaptive dynamics—unpredictable possibilities beyond our control—require far more deliberate instruction and training (Hung, 2008).

Situating Social Cartography

Because global collaborative responses to climate change require reconciling manifold worldviews, intercultural diversity, and interdisciplinary knowledge domains (enumerable and often contested fields of expertise, authorities, and pedagogies), educating for sustainable futures will by definition be rife with conflict. This underscores the need for scholars, researchers, and practitioners not only to experiment with flexible, inclusive, and forgiving theoretical-methodological approaches that help us navigate difficult terrain, competing interests, and differences in perception, but also to embrace conflict for its creative potential. Bastidas and Gonzales (2009) have described social cartography (participatory mapping) "as a tool for the transformation of environmental and social conflicts at the household, community, national, and international levels" (p. 1).

Social cartography has enjoyed a reawakening[2] as a collective knowledge production practice that can broaden the realms and reach of research, analysis, and learning content in response to the increasing complexity, uncertainty, adaptiveness, and interdependence characterizing our lives (Ruitenberg, 2007, 8). Configured as a collaborative research method that gives way to diversified perspectives for understanding the world and phenomena, it can accommodate varied sociocultural, interpersonal, and political experiences, and their influence on subjective, collective, mental, and material realities across time and space. Following on the heels of Welch (1993), education scholars Paulston and Liebman (1994) early on argued in favor of new methods to redress the skewed means by which established conventions of research interpellate culture: disqualifying or misconstruing non-Western cultural understandings. As a democratic participatory knowledge production tool, social cartography seeks broad inclusivity amid multifarious economies of knowledge production, social innovation, and transformation.

Pleas to reconceptualize research methodologies and their knowledge claims aspire toward more reciprocal and nondiscriminatory intercultural relations across education and academics (Paulston & Liebman, 1994). Expanding on what it might mean to apply such a reconceptualization in practice, Paulston (1999) articulated the significance of social cartography for "open[ing] up meanings, . . . uncover[ing] limits within cultural fields, and . . . highlight[ing] reactionary attempts to seal borders and prohibit translations" (as cited in Ruitenberg, 2007, p. 11). Paulston & Liebman (1994) envisioned social cartography as a collaborative device for diversifying knowledge claims and cultural understandings suppressed by dominant hegemonic metanarratives. In succinct words, *social cartography* can be defined as "the art and science of mapping ways of seeing" (Paulston, 1996, p. xv).

Maps are rhetorical images that have traditionally been circumscribed by disciplinary rules and codes that guide cartographic production and applicability (Harley, 1988; Ruitenberg, 2007). In this respect, they confer hefty demarcating sway: maps "never merely represent the world, but always also produce and constitute it" (Ruitenberg, 2007, p. 9). In this book, the concept of mapping and cartography—participatory mapping and social cartography specifically—is used with the broadest meaning in mind: to capture theories and practices of "all forms of mapping, both geographic and non-geographic" (Ruitenberg, 2007, p. 8). Social cartography is conceptualized as a heuristic device for representing more than static, place-based terrain and physicality, to collaboratively discern and understand geographic realities but also nonmaterial phenomena that shift and adapt through time, space and interaction, as captured by graphic depictions, mental maps, flow charts, and other imagery (Ruitenberg, 2007). It comprises a form of provisional, unfolding "visual dialogue" (Paulston & Liebman, 1994), constitutive of co-creative knowledge fields that are "always in the process of becoming" (Kitchin et al., 2013, p. 480).

As an instrument for disrupting engrained conventions of academic knowledge production, the visual dialogue of social cartography enables us to pry open dominant worldviews and belief systems reinscribed time and again, and to probe the deep grammar of discourse engrained within established teleological narrative (Ruitenberg, 2007). Cartographic conceptual analyses thereby facilitate expanded fields of vision beyond textual ordering of time (her/history) to more fully include spatial relations that span culture across scales. In other words, it is intended as a complement to existing methodological tools of textual analysis and scholarship. As Ruitenberg (2007) notes, cartographic discourse [mapping] is not necessarily superior to textual analyses but can assist with the limitations that text and narrative impose. In many instances, provisional social cartography can be more useful for depicting dynamic systems and shifting discourse than "descriptions constrained by words and numbers" (Ruitenberg, 2007, p. 15).

The pivotal role of education, scholarship, and scientific innovation for addressing climate change thrust critical questions with complex answers—based in "unsimple truths" (Mitchell, 2009)—into plain view: education and science according to whom; toward what end; in relation to what measures, values, and criteria; and contextualized within which cultural, political, and ideological perspectives? Comparative (global) education is fraught with debates surrounding such questions, particularly after "the emergence of [the] post-paradigmatic moment" in the 1990s (Gorostiaga, 2017, p. 878; Usarralde, 2006). Social cartography provides a collective medium for conceptually charting and graphically representing this heterodoxic landscape that exists at any given time and that evolves in perpetuity, with the passing of time. As a means to depict, engage, and discern convoluted relations and the "movement of ideas, persons, or social groups in social space" (Ruitenberg, 2007, p. 9), it represents a participatory mapping praxis for collectively engaging the enormous challenges facing us and the planet we inhabit.

In a world saturated with power asymmetries across scope and scale, mapping becomes an important instrument of analysis for navigating unsustainable social systems, structures, and arrangements. The playful methodology of social cartography provides a means to analyze and compare the abundant perspectives at the root of epistemological and existential questions (Gorostiaga, 2017). It lends itself to charting, discerning, and critiquing multidimensional power dynamics—between individuals or social groups, at the center or margins of cultural hegemony. Foremost among the reasons to entertain mapping as a form of transformative visual discourse is the subversive and decolonizing potential it engenders. Moore and Garzón (2010) describe that the maps most people are familiar with as part of early formative schooling "reflect the legacy of colonization, resource extraction, and state control" (p. 67). Although instrumental to colonial processes of reaping resources, Indigenous people today are "at the forefront of using mapping to reclaim their land and resources" (Moore & Garzón, 2010, p. 67).

The need for, yet difficulties of, moving toward more integrated interdisciplinary knowledge production underscores the value of social cartography as a tool for collaborative, cross-fertilizing inquiry. As academic and epistemic structures and systems adjust and transform, we need approaches that facilitate collective "analysis of boundaries and liminal zones, proximity and distance" across the natural and social sciences, the humanities, and the arts, as well as educational theory and research writ large (Ruitenberg, 207, p. 9). Social cartography provides a pathway toward alternative ways of making intelligible what we do not see, know, or understand. Not only does such alternative engagement promote sorely needed transdisciplinary cooperation, it can render more germane collaboration between academic scholars and artists who often exist in isolation. Social cartography opens up opportunities for science and scholarship to draw on and honor artistic faculties in instrumental ways. Brooke Singer's (2007) U.S. Oil Fix map in figure 1.3 on the opposite page provides a graphic representation of the world through the lens of U.S. oil consumption, integrating art, inquiry, and action in one. The map contributes to an atlas on radical cartography (Mogel & Bhagat, 2007), and in the words of the author-artist "is inherently political" (Singer, 2007). It provides an impressionable snapshot in time of the world's foremost consumer of oil in geopolitical relation to regional and national oil reserves across the globe.

Social cartography and mental maps avail us with opportunities to draw, visualize, interpret, communicate, translate, discern, disrupt, deny, organize, reorganize, and more (Kitchin et al., 2013) in ways that literacy and words may not. As Kitchin et al. explain, "they unfold in context through a mix of creative, reflexive, playful, affective and habitual practices; affected by the knowledge, experience and skill of the individual," but also in collaboration with others, who map the world as they perceive it together (p. 481). Andreotti et al. (2016) argue that it is not the maps themselves that allow us to interrupt superimposed understandings or disrupt stubborn delineations, but the act of engaging with them (p. 85). It is the provisionality, creativity, and generative impulse of cartographic conceptual maps that imbue them with value, inviting anyone and everyone to enter into liminal spaces and a collaborative playing field for thinking through, problematizing, accepting, rejecting, or adjusting ways of seeing, sensing, and knowing possible futures.

The map in figure 1.4 provides another example of the cross-fertilizing and generative impulse of conceptual mapping. Paulston's (1994) rendition of knowledge positions in the graphic constellation on page 20 is both subjective and dated, yet highly effective in its capacity to mediate and motivate better understanding of concept relations and conceptual networks.

Other scholars or practitioners may well have arranged the configuration of knowledge positions on this map differently, may have included additional or excluded particular knowledge positions, and may have modified or shifted the focal points. The map was published almost three decades ago and would arguably look different today. Yet analyzing the visual representation encourages the interpreter to contemplate how they might otherwise map the component parts, prompting insight into alternate configurations, and how to otherwise interrelate academic theory,

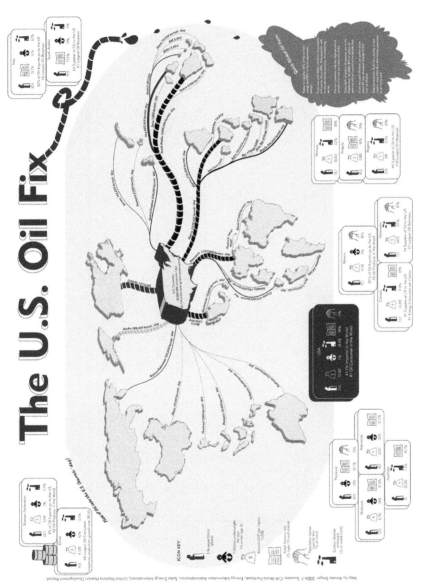

Figure 1.3. The U.S. Oil Fix. *Source:* Singer (2007). Used with permission.

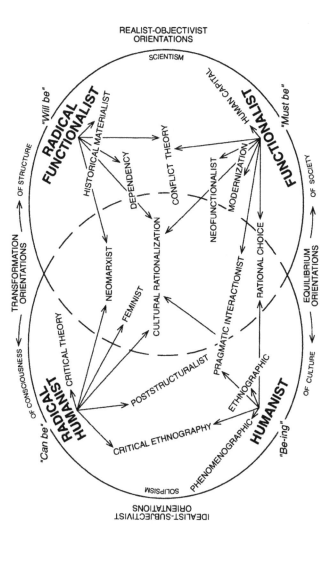

FIG. 2.—With the original caption reading "a macro mapping of paradigms and theories in comparative and international education texts seen as an intellectual field," Paulston's postmodern map opens to all claimants room for inclusion in the social milieu. Source: R. Paulston, "Comparative Education: Paradigms and Theories," in *The International Encyclopedia of Education*, ed. T. Husén and N. Postlethwaite (Oxford: Pergamon, 1994).

Figure 1.4. Macro Mapping of Paradigms and Theories in Comparative Education. *Source:* Paulston (1994, p. 424). Used with permission of Elsevier Science & Technology Journals, conveyed through Copyright Clearance Center, Inc.

discourse, and knowledge. It enables the reader to envision a broader perspective, specifically someone else's perspective at another point in time, of how theoretical orientations and academic scholarship is always provisionally situated, each in relation to the other, and as mediated by shifting time-space configurations.

In sum, social cartography responds to the need for flexible heuristic models that can accommodate complexity, heterodoxy, fluidity, adaptability, and ephemerality. It serves as an expanded form of representation that exists beyond the bounds of unilinear narrative or Euclidean conceptualization. Graphic representations inspired by collaborative, generative processes open up new entry points into dialogue around the pressing issues of our time, widening our range of engagement. They expand the scope and modes of communicating, interacting, and participating in discourse beyond that dominated by narrative text. Equally important, they provide a generative heuristic device that can assist us in breaking down false hierarchies of value related to epistemic authority and legitimacy across culturally contingent science and knowledge accumulation.

Seeds of Sustainability: Braving the Burden of History

> Why would you beat a horse? . . . and how could you not know the horse is dead?
>
> —An idiom in critical perspective

The significance of education for addressing climate change is evidenced by the growing momentum of education for sustainable development (ESD) across world settings (Leicht et al., 2018), and the accompanying policies, practices, and pedagogies that increasingly filter sustainability goals into primary, secondary, and tertiary education. Education for sustainable development is described by Leicht et al. (2018) as empowering learners "to take informed decisions and responsible actions for environmental integrity, economic viability and a just society, for present and future generations, while respecting cultural diversity" (p. 38). But the ability of education to generate the types of responsible action that can sustain earth and its lifeforms is constrained by a persistent need for more critically reflexive, holistic, and counterhegemonic approaches, particularly in reconciling legacies of a problematic past.

Enshrined in the notion of "development" (in ESD), for starters, is the economic reasoning notable scholar-activists argue drives climate change in the first and final instance (de Graaf & Batker, 2011; McKibben, 2010). Many of the models, assumptions, and theories upon which the United Nations (UN) system and its subsidiary organs build, for example, are steeped in contentious history, placing the UN 2030 SDGs in a sobering context. This controversial backdrop has gained increasing recognition as neoliberal globalization accelerates and worldwide disparities continue to widen, processes in which central UN organs like the World Bank and International Monetary Fund are intricately entangled. As a result, folding the UN 2030 SDGs into education requires that we engage critically with the backstories, ideologies, politics, and economics that have deep and far-reaching roots in inequitable social arrangements, and that for many now comprise a "hidden curriculum" of sorts (Anyon, 1980), one that maintains a power structure that does not serve all humans equally or the earth well.

Scholars increasingly recognize historical and ongoing institutional complicity in the violence of coloniality that shape our lives and all life-forms on earth. The analyses in this book build on the work of scholars who critically engage with the lasting impact that colonization and imperialism have had on peoples around the world. As Sheila Nair (2017) has noted, the use of "post" in postcolonial is not meant to suggest that "the effects or impact of colonialism are now long gone" (p. 69). Instead, the deep and far-reaching roots of colonialism, imperialism, and variants of neocolonialism prevail in ways explicit, implicit, buried, and unknown. In particular, I build on and pay special tribute to the remarkable work of Sharon Stein, Vanessa Andreotti, and fellow scholars engaged in unearthing the complex colonial foundations of education, as situated within Western civilizing missions and the inequities of global North-South relations. If we are to imagine and enact alternate sustainable futures, education and learning must enlist decolonization pedagogies and strategies that decipher structural and systemic power dynamics at the global level (Stein et al., 2020, p. 44).

The thread of domination, exploitation, and violence that runs through colonial or imperial histories is one and the same for humans and nonhumans, including nature and the environment. But because interpretations of colonization and decolonization—of lands, people, nature, life on earth—inevitably flow from infinitely varied sources and experiences, social cartography provides a starting point for experimenting with the puzzle of nonprescriptive possibilities that exist outside hegemonic discourse and monocultural deliberation. As Tuck and Yang (2012) have warned, decolonization must beware of becoming another empty metaphor or consumption site for accumulating knowledge currency and acclaim in the economies of Western educational institutions (Stein et al., 2020). Understanding the destructive impact of colonial lifeways for all life on earth requires that we work "with and through complexity, uncertainty, and complicity in order to 'stay with the trouble'" (Haraway, 2016, as cited in Stein et al., 2020, p. 44).

The current climate of decentralized epistemic authority and contested knowledge render all forms of prescriptive diagnosis no more than partial, and encourage flexible, dynamic imaginaries that accommodate diverse claims, including those that contrast or contradict. The Gesturing Towards Decolonial Futures (GTDF) collective references social cartography as a generative, pedagogical tool that can be used to map divergent decolonial theories of change, but that can also be used to flag "traps of inherited colonial habits" that foreclose alternatives to coloniality (Stein et al., 2020, p. 45). Such a collaborative, generative approach is envisioned as an invitation for people to resist deterministic expectations and to instead engage "with the collective tensions, complexities and possibilities that . . . arise at the interface of different critiques, communities, and contrasting onto-metaphysics" (Stein et al., 2020, p. 47).

As visuals that assist us in negotiating the profusion of intellectual orientations, methodologies, and pedagogies generated by the living, the dead, and those yet born, social cartography allows us to make sense of and play with possibilities that emerge from a more inclusive past, plural present, and sentient future—to craft a commons for all life on earth. Understandings about the collective, commons, and communities of belonging, small and large, must address the myth of separability and dehumanization of Others at the core of coloniality. The harm and pain inflicted on people across cultures, countries, and communities stands as a potent reminder and formidable obstacle to a more equitable politics of recognition that fulfills everyone's need for belonging (connection, love, security, purpose, fulfillment, and so forth), no matter where in the world.

To think outside of a (colonial) domination paradigm and notions of an explicitly "*European* world-system" (Eades, 2005, p. 30, italics original) is to re-center the role of world regions cast as peripheral and passive byproducts of Western civilizing creation. It is to reorient the destiny of Western power and hegemony in relation to empires that expand and decline, and to carve spaces where marginalized, silenced, and erased voices can round out the stories we tell. It is to resist superimposing universalizing projections of the world we inhabit together with other humans and other-than-humans, so that we do not enclose ourselves within provincial history and understanding, or delimit visions of possibilities yet to come. Educating for sustainable futures requires that we extend our purview past self-indulgent individualism and the insular present, to widen our frames broad, recollect deep, and fathom far. Following in the footsteps of critical, postcolonial, feminist, antiracist, Indigenous, and decolonization scholars who have taken this charge to task, this is what "otherwise futures" (a.k.a. alternative futures) is intended to denote.

I join fellow scholars who seek to "create a generative, generous, and agnostic space for thinking alongside each other about the future . . . including its challenges, complexities, and possibilities" (Pashby et al., 2021, p. 372). Pashby et al. (2021) note the increasing difficulty scholars and practitioners confront in keeping up with the velocity and course of change. If we are to remain relevant and responsive to the global challenges facing us, the need to revisit and continually revise our methods and approaches to learning is of utmost importance (Pashby et al., 2021). More specifically, the authors invite us to address the "intellectual, affective, and relational economies that frame, enable, and foreclose different educational possibilities" (Pashby et al., 2021, p. 372). This is what a social cartography of soft science sustainability seeks to inspire—a flexible mode of thinking together and relating to each other and the earth that does not foreclose futures, but that instead teases out "otherwise" possibilities displaced by the deeply ingrained vestiges of modern colonial conceptualization (Pashby et al., 2021).

In order to open spaces for dialectical learning, generative modes of knowledge production encourage "border thinking" (Khoo & Jørgensen, 2021), but often at a price ill at ease with academic orthodoxy and its focus on disciplinary depth. This brings to the fore long-standing academic incongruities between depth and breadth of knowledge that tend to siphon each perspective (specialist vs. generalist) off into separate spheres.[3] *Soft Science Sustainability* assembles a broad (though by no means infinite) mosaic of shifting knowledge domains but does not intend or pretend to provide depth of knowledge across fields of expertise. I presage this both as a disclaimer and provocation to venture beyond the borders of conventional academic boundaries, a stance reflected in pleas to expand the horizons of criticality and critical thought toward a more transgressive praxis of border thinking that enacts collaborative and ethical engagement (Khoo & Jørgensen, 2021).

Roadmap for Reading

The social cartography of sustainability competencies explored throughout the pages of this book is intended as more than a prescriptive work in progress. It is an invitation to enter into dialogue about knowledge pluralism, the frames and interpretations we use, and the questions we ask when envisioning the future and its possibilities. The notion of a living inventory of sustainability competencies that shift across three-dimensional moving spheres of a social cartography serves as a guiding reminder of our need to think carefully about the questions we ask and why we ask them, and our need to accept the complexity, unpredictability, and uncertainty they provoke over the fate of our future. At the epicenter of this cartographic cathedral of competency imaginaries is metacognition about the questions we ask and frames we use to guide inquiry. Scholars lament the adverse effects that neoliberal politics have had for commodifying science and research in particular (Pereira & Saltelli, 2017). According to historian Philip Mirowski (1991, 2013), the cumulative corporatization of research has enabled corrupt, self-governed modes of conducting research, undermining impartial pathways to scientific innovation by prioritizing select questions and the framing we use to think about them.

Along similar lines, de Graaf and Batker (2011), in *What's the Economy for Anyway?*, rear-end hallowed questions about "what will that do to the economy?" that deflect attention away from primordial questions about the *fundamental purpose* of the economy. There is little need to worry about the answers, the authors admonish, if "you can get them asking the wrong questions" (Pynchon, 1973, as cited in de Graaf & Batker, 2011, p. 5). Also known as Type III errors that derive from faulty framing and assessing the wrong problem (Kønig et al., 2017), or "hypocognition" (Pereira & Saltelli, 2017) in which knowledge and knowledge production is restrained within normative perspectives, errors in answering the "wrong" questions create "socially constructed ignorance" (Ravetz, 1987; Rayner, 2012; Lakoff, 2010)—what Pereira and Saltelli (2017) characterize as "forced simplification of a complex issue into a simplistic narrative" (p. 56).

The first of the 3Cs spotlight the need to enact intentional, deliberative criticality as part of learning. Introduced in chapter 2, *contemplative criticality* subsumes several core competencies routinely referenced in ESD, including self-awareness, normative, and anticipatory competency. The chapter begins by examining definitions and foundational theory of *critical thinking*, and explores its component parts alongside their instrumentality for advancing counterhegemonic imaginaries. The *contemplative* attribute ascribed to this 3C competency signals the need to slow down, step back, and exercise criticality with mindful and open-minded attention, rather than keep pace with the manic march of efficiency. Like decolonization, "critical thinking" must be more than a buzzword or empty metaphor (Tuck & Yang, 2012). Chapter 2 examines the need for critical reflection to be conceived as multidimensional across scope and scale (i.e. individual, interpersonal, historical, cultural, political) in order to encourage awareness beyond simplistic or insular ideation. As such, the analysis narrows in on criticality as a means to interrogate the foundations and knowledge authorities upon which learning and our assumptions build.

Critical reflexivity requires feedback loops that encourage metacognition about the reinventive impulse of established (modern colonial) ways of being, seeing, and thinking. At the interstices between critical contemplation and the other spheres of sustainability competences (compassionate collaboration, comprehensive complexity) are various vectors that impinge on perception and understanding: the worldviews, knowledge domains, and paradigms we operate with, as well as essential intertemporal considerations—be it short or long range, hindsight or foresight. The remainder of chapter 2 investigates two areas in specific need of careful consideration at this historical juncture: (i) the dark history and lasting legacy of Western colonialism, and (ii) market fundamentalism and the presumed inevitability of neoclassical models of economic reasoning.

Chapter 3, "Compassionate Collaboration," draws attention to the vital need for cooperative approaches in crossing the infinite divides that separate us across scope and scale (nation, race, ethnicity, religion, discipline, and so on). Investing in alternative sustainable lifeways will require concerted efforts to transcend entrenched notions of human (and other-than-human) separability, fragmentation and atomization. Toward this end, the chapter homes in on two areas directly related to education as a point of departure. The first section explores the meanings and applicability of interdisciplinarity as situated within contemporary institutions of higher education. The difficulties of engaging in cross-disciplinary fertilization within higher education remain legion and are discouraged by deeply rooted institutional mechanisms that force academics to prioritize less risky endeavors in securing promotion and academic tenure. This typically results in far less interdisciplinary collaboration than is needed and serves as a bad example for modeling to students an increasingly crucial criteria in efforts to address climate change.

The second section of chapter 3 critically examines global citizenship education (GCE) and critical inclusive education as areas of expertise that seek to engage citizens around the world and forge cooperation across sociocultural difference and ethnic belonging. The analysis explores the role of civic learning and democratic engagement within these fields of education in contemporary times. Chapter 3 concludes with the importance of GCE for connecting the global-local and local-global. Notions of global citizenship must be grounded in place-based community and human relations that centerstage compassion and care, while connecting (mapping) diverse perspectives and generative knowledge to global systems and forces. To a large degree, this involves connecting learning to the world outside the classroom, or moving the classroom out into the world.

Chapter 4 explores the significance of complexity, interacting adaptive systems, and knowledge uncertainty. The chapter begins by defining "wicked problems" and their multidimensional, unstable, and ambiguous attributes, before expounding on the flexibility and fluency in cognitive and metacognitive reasoning needed to tackle complexity. In the first section, the chapter examines systems thinking and problem-solving competency that seeks *not* to solve problems, but to re-solve them time and again. Emphasis is placed on how problems are conceptualized and framed, with particular focus on the role that diversified theories, paradigms, and models have for alternative ways of seeing, thinking, and understanding phenomena. Chapter 4 next introduces the popularized concepts used to characterize the current global landscape, captured by the acronym VUCA: volatility, uncertainty, complexity, and ambiguity.

The VUCA vocabularies encapsulate our unsettled sense of, and growing preoccupation with accelerating change, uncertainty, and complexity as the twenty-first century unfolds. Chapter 4 explores the definitions and meanings of VUCA, before critically engaging dominant perspectives that continue to present the world as objectively measurable, predictable, and controllable. False imaginaries of certainty and exactitude lend a sense of security and have long provided a means of (colonial) control through classification and taxonomies, and although the rationalities and logic around which this control is structured has become "intimately biopolitical" (Shotwell, 2016) as part of modern lifeways (i.e., race, gender, sexuality, etc.), they build on and maintain established foundations of oppression and violence. In sum, the hierarchies of domination and ownership that differentially value and devalue groups of people and species on earth require careful analysis and deconstruction, while the realities of uncertainty and things unknown demand patience and acquiescence.

As the hallmark of twenty-first-century education, global dialectical learning must guide efforts to transcend narrow, additive, or absolute reasoning, and strive to infuse adaptive systems thinking, complexity, and knowledge uncertainty into multicultural, deliberative forms of knowledge accumulation. Such diverse and dynamic forms of sustainability education demand higher thresholds for ambiguity, flexibility in learning and pedagogy, and reflexive analysis of what it means to live in a local-global world amid sociopolitical insecurity and conflicting narratives about climate change, a world in which the existence of facts are disputed and polarized versions of truth reign. Dialectical learning is prey to the cynical realities of despoiled truth, including insidious, multilayered appropriation tactics: fake news, false arguments, alternative facts, distorted science, reconstructed histories, troll factories, and "asymmetries of passion" that play out across social media in filter bubbles (Kakutani, 2018; DiResta, 2018).

Not only do the sifted siloes that virtual life amplify evade counter-content—with a dearth of information to juxtapose the zealous views of extremist groups committed to their cause (DiResta, 2018)—the rise of "truth decay" and inside-out alternative realities employ the "disturbing Orwellian trick . . . of using words to mean the exact opposite of what they really mean" (Kakutani, 2018, para. 36), all in order "to assert power over reality [truth] itself" (Gessen, 2016, as cited in Kakutani, 2018, para. 39). The factual anarchy we find ourselves amid makes for difficult terrain within which to situate dialectical learning and critique. Contextualized within the controversial polarization that configures contemporary times, questions about the meanings of national citizenship in a global world facing planetary crisis become a moot point when confronted with those who deny climate change altogether. There are no simple answers to these and like dilemmas—indeed they are precisely part and parcel of the problems facing us.

Chapter 5 concludes the book by returning to the transformative potential of education for creating a sustainable, inclusive world community. Scholars note that efforts to bring about sustainable futures "that continue to separate humans from the rest of the world are delusional and futile" (Taylor et al., 2020, p. 1). In order to move toward sustainable and equitable lifeways for humans and other-than-humans, transformative education must venture outside modern colonial habits of seeing, being, and sensing. In order to bring all humans and other-than-humans into the orbit of transformative change, discourse and dialogue must reconcile the harmful dislocations that violence and oppression leave behind. The significance of transgenerational trauma and collective healing in moving us toward sustainable lifeways is explored as part of the analysis. The final chapter thus returns to the significance of history for reckoning with and reconciling harms, both past and persistent, perpetrated against peoples, lands, and life on earth.

Chapter Two

Contemplative Criticality and Unlearning

Toward Anticolonial Sustainability

Although "it is human nature to think," it is "not natural for humans to think well" according to critical thinking scholar Richard Paul (Elder, 2010, p. 2). There are endless reasons why humans might not think "well" or critically: fatigue, fear, privation, pain, shame, benefit, and bias are a few. Despite the ubiquity of human thought—pervading "every aspect of human life and every dimension of the human mind"—there are powerful forces that shelter us from perceived threat, preserve comforting or desired perspectives, and distort perception: "prejudice, illusion, mythology, ignorance, and self-deception" (Elder, 2010, p. 2). Denial and delusion in particular are potently effective, and in many cases indispensable defense mechanisms, that can intrude upon critical thinking. For these reasons and more, metacognition that hones the ability to analyze, evaluate, and interrupt rote thinking is crucial. In this chapter, critical thinking and reflection is understood as a gateway competency upon which all learning necessarily builds. It is the source of lifelong learning writ large, and a core ingredient at the base of every educational endeavor. By its most expansive definition, critical reflection begins the day we are born.

The field of critical thinking is vast and complex, and attached to varied meanings that take their lead from different focal points. Although its deepest Western intellectual roots are often traced to Socrates thousands of years ago, the modern critical-thinking movement remained "no more than a small, scattered group of educators" as late as the mid-1980s (Paul, 1993, p. 38). Concerned with the rigid and didactic stronghold of formal learning, educators and advocates began pushing toward Socratic instruction and a more robust reflexive education paradigm. Despite the ultimate triumph of critical thinking as a bastion of learning (at least in theory), its application remains evasive and difficult to "operationalize" and, more problematically, to evaluate according to modern metrics.

Yet if the steady stream of assessment rubrics, templates, guidelines, and professional development are any indication, critical thinking has without doubt become the mainstay of education praxis. This despite the dismal reports of students who graduate deficient in analytical skills and critical thinking proficiency, however (Arum & Roksa, 2011). The problem, in part, is that critical thinking is most effectively cultivated in communities of learning that facilitate meaningful (sincere) experiential interaction and requires resources that are increasingly scarce (i.e., small class size, time to deliberate). The marker *contemplative* in this 3C competency represents the need to avoid performative praxis that reduce criticality to hollow hallmarks, or mindfulness to a corporate tool of social control (i.e., McMindfulness). It signals the need to slow down and reclaim our "stolen focus" so we can "think deeply again" (Hari, 2022).

In the U.S., education has a long history of anti-intellectualism according to Paul (1993), with a narrow focus on "passive learning, lower-order training, and indoctrination" (p. 37). Paul is not alone, in the U.S. or elsewhere, in exposing the indoctrinating thrust and intent of educating the populace (Freire, 2010; Anyon, 1980; Giroux & Purpel, 1983). Building on the early Paulian tradition that developed prior to the 1990s, critical-thinking scholars began directing attention to the influence of bias in human thinking, including the "pervasive role of egocentric and sociocentric tendencies . . . [as] significant barriers to the development of critical capacities" (Elder, 2010, p. 6). Because every subject, discipline, and domain of human inquiry is a mode of thinking susceptible to bias, knowledge must always be understood in relation to the elements of reasoning within which it is embedded. Many models for navigating the tricky terrain associated with self-reflection, cultural reflexivity, and critical deconstruction exist, each contributing value to the registers that broaden human and other-than-human understanding.

For critical-thinking trailblazer Stephen Brookfield (2012), the realm of cognition and thought susceptible to bias is linked to thinking framed by our assumptions and that determine action. Thinking critically is to question dominant ideologies and approaches we internalize as part of the social constructs, political hegemony, and power dynamics at the base of culture and enculturation. To think critically is to identify these assumptions, determine the degree to which they hold validity, and to examine our personal, intellectual, and organizational ideas and perceptions before making decisions or taking action (Brookfield, 2012, p. 1). Brookfield distinguishes three types of assumptions: paradigmatic, prescriptive, and causal. Paradigmatic assumptions are "structuring assumptions we use to order the world into fundamental categories" (Brookfield, 2012, p. 17). Because we typically fail to recognize these categories as assumptions (social constructs) and unconsciously presume (even insist on) their objectivity and legitimacy, they are the most difficult to discern (Brookfield, 2012, p. 17).

Grounded in paradigmatic assumptions are *prescriptive assumptions* that pertain to "what we think ought to be happening in a particular situation" (Brookfield, 2012, p. 18). These are assumptions that implicate ideas and everyday suppositions about how people *"should* behave, [or] what . . . processes *should* look like" (Brookfield, p. 18, italics mine). Closer to the surface, they are easier to discern. *Causal assumptions,* finally, relate to our understandings of "how different parts of the world work and . . . the conditions under which these can be changed" (Brookfield, 2012, p. 18). They are the easiest of Brookfield's trifecta of assumptions to unearth, and in turn are classified into (1) predictive assumptions that guide behavior versus (2) retroactive assumptions, which rely on past experience to guide future conduct (p. 19). No matter how assumptions are "typed" or "classified," they are "rarely right or wrong" (Brookfield, 2012, p. 19). Instead, their appropriateness is determined in relation to the conditions and context within which they are situated. Broadening the scope of these contingencies outward across scale, from the personal distinctive to the universal global (cross-species included), assumptions remain forever captive to the particulars and partiality of perspective—in the eyes of the beholder.

Scholars have developed critical-thinking models for generating, deepening, and documenting learning, and for facilitating proactive responsibility in learning (Ash and Clayton, 2009). Ash and Clayton's (2009) model for instance, known by its acronym DEAL (describe, examine, and articulate learning), guides students to learn and think critically with mindful intention by examining their knowledge and identifying its validity (and gaps), using evidence. Students are directed to describe the learning activities they engage in with attention to purpose and detail, before proceeding to critically reflect on and examine their learning experience. DEAL's second step—examine learning—specifically directs students to identify interlinkages between learning objectives and their personal experiences. The model encourages learning that leads to action, which the authors believe is proactively facilitated when students are empowered to articulate their own personal learning process.

The critical reflection approaches described above resonate with the reflective competencies commonly referenced throughout education for sustainable development (self-awareness, normative, anticipatory), and emphasize the need to include in learning deliberations the experience(s) each of us bring to knowledge production—from the individual and personal to the collective and cultural, extending backward in time or across different dimensions of our lives (personal, familial, professional, political, religious, etc.). In this social cartography (see figure 2.1 below), contemplative criticality subsumes all three critical reflection competencies identified as integral to sustainability education (ESD).

According to Leicht et al. (2018), the *normative competency* of ESD coheres around the ability to recognize, reflect on, and understand the values and norms that influence behavior, and to navigate differing

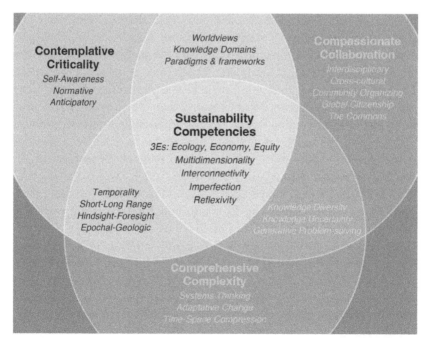

Figure 2.1. 3C Contemplative Criticality Diagram. *Source*: Created by the author.

values, principles, goals, and targets related to sustainability. The authors further describe *anticipatory competency* as "the ability to understand and evaluate multiple futures—possible, probable and desirable—and to create one's own visions of the future" (Leicht et al., 2018, p. 44). This speaks to the intertemporal dimension of criticality, since our sense of the future is difficult to dislodge from our experiences of the past and present (more on this below).

As a recent buzzword in organizational leadership and management, *self-awareness* competency warrants specific attention. The Oxford Languages dictionary definition of *self-awareness* is "conscious knowledge of one's own character, feelings, motives, and desires." The concept has proved ambiguous to define concisely, however, with researchers deferring to varied versions over the past half century (Eurich, 2018). Despite its proclaimed significance in facilitating communication, strengthening relationships, and encouraging sound decision-making, moreover, we know "surprisingly little about improving this critical skill" according to organizational psychologist Tasha Eurich (2018, para. 2). Based on a large-scale, ongoing scientific study of self-awareness, Eurich found that despite what most people believe about themselves, self-awareness is relatively rare: only 10–15 percent of those studied actually met the requisite criteria.

Self-awareness theory was first established as a veritable field of study within psychology in the early 1970s. The landmark publication by Duval and Wicklund (1972) emphasized the human capacity to self-reflect on and evaluate our behavior in juxtaposition to internal values and standards. In other words, self-awareness implies metacognitive ability to recognize and contemplate our internal thoughts and sense of self, and compare these to our outward-facing identity. According to Eurich (2018), two broad categories have emerged across research on self-awareness. *Internal self-awareness* pertains to "how clearly we see our own values, passions, aspirations, fit with our environment, reactions (including thoughts, feelings, behaviors, strengths, and weaknesses), and impact on others" (Eurich, 2018, para. 6). *External self-awareness* denotes our understanding of other people's perception of us, in relation to the same factors outlined above (Eurich, 2018). This dual characterization has particular implications for people with power or in leadership positions, who are most successful in their role when able to balance the competing viewpoints of both *internal* and *external* self-awareness.

A telling pattern has emerged in the correlation between power and self-perception: the more power leaders acquire, the more likely they are to overestimate their abilities and skills (Eurich, 2018). This is because the higher up the power ladder a leader climbs, the fewer people there are in a position to provide honest, critical feedback. As a result, the unconscious thoughts, feelings, and motives that drive the decisions and behavior of leaders often go unchecked. This can become especially acute if effective mechanisms are not in place to safeguard against overreactions to critique, if there are few colleagues with whom to "gut-check" unexpected or challenging feedback (Eurich, 2018). As Eurich (2018) concludes, "because so much is trapped outside our conscious awareness, we tend to invent answers that *feel* true but are often wrong" (para. 20). When wielding power over decision-making, the adverse effects of faulty self-perception and bad decisions will increase intact with the number of people involved. All this to say that with power comes great responsibility, and that critical self-awareness—facilitated by external feedback loops—is indispensable if we aspire toward more equitable power relations.

The three foundational critical reflection competencies (self-awareness, normative, anticipatory) explored above and common to ESD overlap in instrumental ways but are also significantly imbued with intertemporality. Our experiences of the present and consequent vision of the future, with its possibilities, are fundamentally mediated by the past –by our experiences of who we are as situated within lived experience, but also within histories and genealogies, and the values, norms, and traditions with which we are enculturated. Karl Marx's (1994) renowned quote that men [sic] make history "under circumstances existing already, given and transmitted from the past" and that "the tradition of all dead generations weighs like a nightmare on the brains of the living" captures the weight of historical hindsight for the present and future (p. 4). Although mainstream narratives of history overwhelmingly centerstage heroes and the victors, truth and "unforgetting" (Dunbar-Ortiz, 2008) seeks to transcend partial or sanitized portraits of the past and to restore realities omitted.

In other words, critical reflection must strive toward multidimensionality across scope and scale (individual, interpersonal, social, historical, political, cultural—the list goes on), and must be charged with more than activating individual self-awareness or students' ability to recognize their position in historical and cultural context. It is incumbent upon institutions of higher education (the human agents governing its structures and principles) which "developed alongside and through colonialism, and remain[s] structurally dependent upon colonialism" (Stein, 2019a, p. 198), to critically (self)reflect on the foundations and knowledge authorities upon which they build. We must prepare students to become gatekeepers, armored with creative ability to disrupt the persistence and repetition of coloniality. As noted above, the *contemplative* attribute ascribed to this 3C *criticality* competency signals the need to slow down, step back, and exercise critical thinking with mindful presence and careful deliberation, rather than move through prescribed motions in mind-numbing monotony.

Politics, Power, and Criticality

In depicting her creative writing process for a book project, Lisa (Leigh) Patel (2014) eloquently describes the "deep pauses that held [her] corpus of work at bay" (p. 357). As she explains, pausing is important, even necessary, but from the perspective of Western colonizing frameworks it is considered bad. Pauses signal missed deadlines, or that "someone elsewhere [may be] writing while [you] are not" (Patel, 2014, p. 357). Slowing down and stepping back, and allowing ourselves the reprieve to collect our thoughts, reflect, or simply feel has become increasingly prohibitive in "modern times in which colonial projects have shaped technology, knowledge, and connection to be a veritable nonstop stimulation of tweets, status updates, and deadlines, all competing for our attention" (Patel, 2014, p. 357; Lanham, 2006). Quieting our minds and pausing production, in order to learn while expectations are interrupted, allow innovative alternatives to competitive learning and established knowledge authority to take shape (Patel, 2014). It further forces us to model what learning might look outside the stranglehold of hollow productivity and a "seemingly unrelenting quest for data [and] publications" (Patel, 2014, p. 357).

In *Cultivating Genius*, literacy scholar Gholdy Muhammad (2020) includes criticality as a central criteria of her four-layered Historically Responsive Literacy (HRL) framework. For Muhammad (2020), *criticality* is defined in relation to reading, writing, and thinking that links to understandings of power, oppression, and social justice. This is particularly important for historically marginalized groups of people (Muhammad, 2020). Her definition extends the concept of thinking critically beyond skills and measurable benchmarks common to academic assessment. The VALUE (Valid Assessment of Learning in Undergraduate Education) rubrics developed by the American Association of Colleges and Universities (AAC&U) for instance, defines *critical thinking* as "a habit of mind characterized by the comprehensive exploration of issues, ideas, artifacts, and events before accepting or formulating an opinion or conclusion" (AAC&U, n.d.). Not necessarily intended as an exhaustive assessment tool, the strength of the AAC&U definition includes its broad reach in consolidating essential learning outcomes across diverse disciplines, fields of study, campuses, institutions, and learning pathways. The rubric's criteria does not, however, rise to the level of specificity featured in Muhammad's framework and learning goals in relation to power and inequity.

AAC&U's Critical Thinking VALUE Rubric defines ability to contextualize (phenomena) as examining our own and other people's assumptions and carefully considering the impact of context when formulating a position (AAC&U, n.d.). *Context*, in turn, is defined as "the historical, ethical, political, cultural, environmental, or circumstantial settings or conditions that influence and complicate the consideration of any issues, ideas, artifacts, and events" (AAC&U, n.d.). Although perhaps implicit as part of "ethics," "politics," and the "conditions" that complicate matters, the rubric nowhere specifies power and privilege as central benchmark features. Considering that power relations loom large in life, and that "we have never had a world free from oppression" (Muhammad, 2020), the need for pedagogy that specifically engages student criticality related to power, privilege, inequity, and oppression is noteworthy. If we wish to cultivate agency that inspires social transformation and to build a better world, students must be able to identify, interrogate, and understand injustice (Muhammad, 2020). Muhammad differentiates between *critical* with a lowercase c, and *Critical* with an uppercase C, to pinpoint this significant distinction in cultivating criticality and agency.

Without deliberately engaging anti-oppressive knowledge, beliefs, and learning, as understood from the perspectives, worldviews, and ideologies of marginalized communities themselves, Criticality remains incomplete. Criticality is being able to feel "for those who are not treated in humane ways regardless of what the law, policy, or norms dictate" (Muhammad, 2020, p. 120). It is not a time filler or add-on curricular activity used when other learning content is completed. It systematically directs our gaze and intellectual faculties toward understanding "the state of humanity" (Muhammad, 2020, p. 132). Criticality is not passive learning, but rather is grounded in students' authentic identities and self-actualization, and agitation that seeks to "upset, disturb, disquiet, and unhinge systemic oppression" (p. 125). More than technical skills and literacy, Criticality requires that we ask ourselves what our responsibilities are in response to violence and oppression perpetrated against other humans (Muhammad, 2020). What does it mean to be human or other-than-human, by extension, in a world where environmental injustice presents a formidable threat to our existence, for instance?

A great deal of anti-oppressive educational resources currently exist with the goal of social change in mind—in the tradition of critical theory, pedagogy, and praxis—and are already in circulation among scholars committed to transformative education. Yet because they are subject to the reinventive thrust of prevailing Eurocentric approaches, social change efforts within education must filter throughout learning reflexive feedback mechanisms that disrupt the tendency of modern colonial lifeways and habits to replicate (Stein, 2020). Sustainability education must build on strength-based approaches that integrate practices from across existing curricula and knowledge domains, all while encouraging metacognition about the recursive and appropriating menace of modern coloniality.

The remainder of this chapter explores two areas in particular need of careful deliberation and agitation literacy, in order to unsettle deeply sedimented educational hegemonies. The first involves the long arch and lasting legacy of Western colonialism, with its far-reaching impact for structuring our lives, being, and ways of knowing. As Stein (2016) notes, there "is not one contemporary campus issue that isn't shaped by [colonial logic]" (p. 2) in higher education. The second area could readily be subsumed within the first but because of its instrumentality as an organizing principle of colonial projects, deserves expounding in its own right: economic fundamentalism and the presumed inevitability of (neo) classical models as the only viable, universal path of economic reasoning. Each of these are examined in the sections that follow.

Unforgetting His Story, Countering Coloniality

The master's tools will never dismantle the master's house.

—Audre Lorde

Conquest and coloniality is the master narrative that runs through the long arch of domination and control in the Anthropocene. It is more than an origin story or historical event in dispersed global settings and persists as a form of "material structure and ordering logics" (Stein, 2016, para.

2) sedimented throughout a global geopolitical system that we take for granted (Stein, 2016; Rowe & Tuck, 2016). If we take seriously how fundamentally and profoundly colonization has shaped our social arrangements, institutions, and public imagination, we can appreciate decolonization as "a complex and contested process of unlearning and undoing centuries of colonial ideas, desires, infrastructures, and of (re)learning how to be in the world together differently" (Stein, 2017, para 2). Unlearning coloniality, in this context, will take careful, critical contemplation, and must inevitably disrupt the very foundations upon which education and learning traditionally build. This, in large part, is the challenge inscribed in the plea for education to change. When UNESCO concludes that education must change if it is to effectively address climate change—that it must be "flexible, culturally sensitive, relevant and suited to changing people's values and behaviors" (World We Want, 2013, iv)—the burden of unlearning coloniality, whether in mind or matter, is part and parcel of the disruption required.

As the legacy and residual catalyst of Western (neo)imperialism, coloniality and modernization have increasingly extended into the far reaches of contemporary life across the globe, disrupting local lifeways and subsistence culture. Coloniality was built on the premise that those who wield power are entitled to control, dominate, and exploit to their advantage all living and nonliving matter at their disposal (land, resources, animals, humans, culture, etc.), without regard for harms inflicted. Decolonization processes necessitate deconstructing our notions of the historical practices and assumptions that live on in the present and that sustain colonial processes under the rubric "development" and "modernization," in the name of "progress." We need to develop educational tools, pedagogies, and curricula that explicitly recognize the means by which coloniality has oppressed, exploited, and dominated peoples, places, and practices—including our imaginaries—with lasting impact. In other words, the particulars and persistence of historic colonization (specific to each location) must be examined in relation to modernization and development theories—as the zeitgeist of "universal progress" in the era of modernity. Offshoots of the Western modernization model pervade contemporary reasoning, including the rationalities that structure economic globalization and its endless growth model, modern science with its foci on separation and dichotomies (public-private divide, gender binary, atomized individualism), and contemporary global North-South relations.

In the introductory chapter of *Against Purity*, Alexis Shotwell (2016) argues that the land and place grabs central to colonialism involved "relations more than they . . . [did] locations" (p. 23). This seemingly simple observation beholds a world filled with infinite possibilities for alternative lifeways. Colonization and nation-state building, with its classification ordering, became a dominant and destructive lifeway that systematically sought to erase all "other" ways of life, including memories of such erasure. Critical reflection demands deliberate engagement with the histories, afterlife, and persistence of coloniality, engagement that allows the global community to reconcile how colonial systems—and ways of knowing, thinking, and being— have fundamentally come to configure life on earth. This must include candid reckoning with the central role of market fundamentalism and historic resource racketeering in the "Capitalocene" (Shotwell, 2016), with its largely uncontested master narratives about scarcity, competition, and the presumed inevitability of neoliberal economic globalization. As a derivative of Western modernization rationality, the neoliberal world order has colonized the imagination to such an extent that, for many, alternative thinking has become unthinkable. For others, in turn, life is simply so burdened by managing day to day—working long and overwhelming hours, caring for children and family members in need, alleviating rising rates of anxiety and depression—that there is little time for reflective thinking of any kind.

At the ground level, contemplative criticality requires interrupting ethnocentric perspectives of modernization that rationalize coloniality and that historically established inequitable arrangements to the benefit of Western powers as part of global geopolitical developments. Beyond the historical particulars in disparate locations, interrogating colonialism involves questioning deep-rooted definitions of "development" and "progress," and their persistent entanglement in unfair trade agreements, the debt trap, and aid industries that maintain flows of money from poor countries in the global South to rich countries in the global North. Contemplative criticality, moreover, insists that we pose questions rather than profess solutions, that we inspire self-reflection (individual, sociocultural, national), skepticism, and humility, rather than preemptive confidence and conviction. It insists that we ask how we can reconcile harms inflicted and amend for the lasting impact of colonization in cultures across global place, space, and diaspora. Contemplative criticality therefore insists that we invest in an economics of reconciliation (i.e., reparations, truth and reconciliation commissions, etc.) in order to redress the lasting impact of historical colonial narratives in relation to widening inequities across the world.

Pushing back against the current trend of anti-intellectualism, education must strive to move beyond ahistorical, decontextualized, depoliticized, and disembodied accounts, in efforts to reestablish agency, politics of power, history, and context, as well as affect and emotion, as integral components of learning, knowledge accumulation, and theorizing. Using critical pedagogy, a central learning objective should include questioning mainstream liberal and neoliberal doxa and practices inherent in established fields of study, and emergent across higher education, so that students learn to question received wisdom, interrogate the histories they inherit, and self-reflect on their place and social role in the world. Toward this end, curricula should aim to weave together critical theory (i.e., feminist, critical race, queer, postcolonial and post-structural, etc.) that denaturalize presumed givens about the world across programs of study and, indeed, all learning. Vanessa Andreotti's (2015) HEADS UP checklist of historical colonial patterns provides a curricular guide and starting point for interrogating the persistent asymmetries of global North-South relations, for instance, and their unacknowledged connections to knowledge production across education.

The HEADS UP acronym corresponds with seven historical colonial patterns as described by Andreotti (2015, pp. 223–224) and serves as a checklist:

> **H**egemonic (justifying superiority and exceptionalism)
> **E**thnocentric (projecting one view, one "forward," one idea of development, as universal)
> **A**historical (forgetting historical legacies and complicities)
> **D**epoliticized (disregarding power inequalities and ideological roots of analysis)
> **S**elf-congratulatory and self-serving (oriented toward self-affirmation and C.V. building)
> **U**ncomplicated solutions (offering easy solutions that do not require systemic change)
> **P**aternalism (seeking affirmation of superiority through the provision of help)

The HEADS UP checklist was developed to counter the deep-seated legacy of a (mythic) universal narrative superimposed onto diverse peoples around the world: the "dominant modern/colonial global imaginary based on a single story of progress, development and human evolution that ascribes differentiated value to cultures/countries that are perceived to be 'behind' in history and time and cultures/countries perceived to be 'ahead'" (Andreotti, 2015, p. 222).

Andreotti references existing scholarship devoted to this educational phenomenon (Willinsky, 1998; Baaz, 2005; Le Heron & Lewis, 2007; Andreotti, 2011a; Abdi & Shultz, 2008; Shultz, 2007; Tallon & McGregor, 2014) and the insidious power that a singular narrative of progress and development has had in capturing "our collective imagination and desires in ways that are extremely difficult to identify, let alone interrupt" (2015, p. 2). Whether we invoke Bourdieu's (1977) notion of habitus or Freudian analysis of libidinally bound imaginaries-cum-behavior, modern colonial constructs and their narratives (e.g., nationalism, materialism, consumerism, narcissism) provide a "(false) sense of stability, fulfillment and satisfaction . . . (e.g., sense of belonging, community, togetherness, prestige, heroism, and pride)" (Andreotti, 2015, p. 5) in ways we are unaware of. In other words, a whole host of culturally contingent, unconscious registers, desires (human needs), and (humanitarian) fantasies circumscribe the way we think and act (Andreotti, 2015, p. 5). Education, scholarship, activism, and advocacy, moreover, have long revealed the tendency for inequities to reproduce despite efforts to the contrary. It is in this context that Andreotti (2015) urges permanent vigilance, questioning, and compassion in discerning "our wider complicity and vested interests in social hierarches and principles of separability" that seemingly reinvent the same patterns we seek to redress, while heralding transformation (p. 4).

Historically responsive and reflexive curricular resources like this provide proactive guideposts for learning from history, in order to avoid repeating harmful social arrangements and relations. They serve as heuristic teaching-learning devices so that we may help students, as future leaders, identify and interrupt the reproduction of paradigms that resurface time and again to the detriment of people and the planet. How do global politics of identity and hierarchies of belonging, which position groups of people against each other, factor into the need to generate dialogue and a common agenda for humanity and planet earth? In what ways do politics of identity intersect with people's differing experiences of life and livelihood amid pressing climate change? Above all, in what ways can the economic thrust and drive characterizing the Capitalocene (Shotwell, 2016) be assuaged, and vulgar economic determinism be reimagined, so that humans and nonhumans can live, thrive, and survive together on planet earth?

Market Fundamentalism: (Re)embedding the Economy

> The power of the fossil fuel industry is so great that, like a giant star, it warps the gravity of everything around it.
>
> —Bill McKibben

In many regards, the economy is the most urgent of all sectors where transformation is needed. Listed in *The Future Is Now* (United Nations, 2019) as a main entry point for transformation, economics (finance) is positioned as one among numerous, seemingly equal levers of change that require action if we are to solve the compounding problems associated with climate change. It has become increasingly clear to many scholars and activists, however, that the economy is *the* driving force, if not root cause, of complex, globally interconnected issues facing us. An infusion of alternative economic models that balance the scales (across various measures) are needed but have long been disqualified by neoclassical economic theory, market determinism, and private sector interests. In recent years, "new economics" has gained traction among academics and advocates across world settings, and young scholar activists in particular have begun mobilizing against the paralyzing stronghold of neoliberal economic reasoning. New economics injects hope into the otherwise sense of impossibility that alternatives are possible. The Illuminator[1] message in the image on the opposite page, projected outside the 2015 American Economic Association (AEA) annual conference, provides a powerful visual of the subversive energies that has emerged among this new class of economists.

Colonial conquest, domination, oppression, and exploitation (of resources, humans, and nonhumans) cannot be divorced from the *longue durée* of a global capitalist economic system and its recursive force. Celebrated scholars have detailed the impact of global capitalism for human life within and across localities, for creating the conditions that maintain neocolonial servitude and oppression among and between peoples differentially positioned along North-South geopolitical divides (Beckert, 2014; Castells, 2010; Harvey, 2005; Sachs, 2015; Smith, 2004; Wallerstein, 2004). In "Slavery and Capitalism" (2014) Harvard historian Sven Beckert reviews

Figure 2.2. Illuminator's Message Outside the AEA 2015 Annual Conference. *Source*: "Is Economic Growth Killing the Planet?," January 2015, The Illuminator Collective. Used with permission.

with sweeping clarity the verdict advanced by a younger class of American historians (i.e., Walter Johnson, Seth Rockman, Caitlin Rosenthal, Edward Baptist): that slavery and enslavement was integral to American capitalism and the expansion of modern industry. For Johnson (2013) it was more than integral to capitalism, it was its very essence (Beckert, 2014, para. 8). Related arguments counter the economics of colonizing natural lands, resources, and the commons that build on notions of the earth and all things earthly as forms of private property, available first come, first served or by survival of the fittest (Naess, 1973; Kallis, 2018; Sessions, 2014).

As important as reports like *The Future Is Now* are, and as crucial as the United Nations remains as the only international intergovernmental body around which world nations might unite, critical and reflexive engagement with the history and global reach of racial capitalism (Robinson, 1983; Kelley, 2022; Gilmore, 2022) cannot remain peripheral to advancing a sustainable future. It necessarily demands that we critically reflect on and recognize the central role of the United Nations and its subsidiary organs as part of this global geopolitical history. To achieve a sustainable future we must heed the warning signs that deep historical analyses reveal. Reconceptualizing our economic system, or simply envisioning alternative possibilities, has for too long and by default been perceived as fantasy, "no more practical than time travel" in the words of *Guardian* reporter Andy Beckett (2019).

An increasing number of scholars and experts across industries and fields of study are directing attention to "new" or alternative economics in efforts to move beyond notions of the economy as an abstract, objective science based on rational calculations and value-free transactions. "New economics" comprises varied streams of thought and nascent think tanks that focus attention on themes that resonate across sustainability curricula. The British new economics think tank Common Wealth, for instance, includes among their goals to develop "institutions that are democratic by design, inclusive in action, and social in purpose," something that will require systemic change and alternative understandings of ownership (over land, resources, peoples, animals), as well as reckoning with the fraught relationships between capital, accumulation by dispossession, and aspirations of democracy (Common Wealth, n.d.).

The U.S.-based Institute for New Economic Thinking (INET) similarly outlines its principles for envisioning a new economic order, including, inter alia, that economists must operate independently of powerful interests; that economic systems are not predictable equations but are characterized by (human) complexity and uncertainty; that growth and productivity should not surpass equality and distribution of resources in significance; that alternative models to neoclassical orthodoxy, alongside diversity and heterodoxy of perspectives, are essential to intellectual growth and innovation; that (deep) history is central to understanding; and that siloed specialization limits our full understanding of the issues confronting us. These new economic perspectives parallel insights that surface throughout ESD and sustainability curricula, and point toward the destructive tour de force of *Homos economicus* for climate change. They confirm the need to (re)envision the economy as embedded within social relations and planetary boundaries, as a system that serves people, society, and planet earth, rather than enabling power grabs and capital accumulation among a privileged few.

Joining the rising tide of new economics and emerging paradigm shift in thinking is the increased influence of women in a field long dominated by males. In *Unbound: How Inequality Constricts Our Economy and What We Can Do About It*, Heather Boushey (2019), of the Washington

Center for Equitable Growth, notes that women are contributing some of the most significant research on the negative impact of inequality for economic development. These female standpoint and feminist economics are not in themselves new. Nor are they a defunct sideshow with their tired gaze on gendered externalities like domestic labor, care-work, and the political economy of reproduction. They are about more than the stubborn gender pay gap, glass ceiling, and triple shift. They are about confronting the shallow inadequacy of economics engineered by and for men, in the form of global racial and patriarchal capitalism, that fails to account for all null and void economic externalities because it abstracts economic transactions from social life and relations. The question of how "new" or not these strains of thinking in economics are can be debated but is irrelevant. Relevant is what we now do, within a rapidly shrinking window of opportunity, to envision and put into action humanely fair and economically sound alternatives in which people and life on earth matter.

Notions of both economic embeddedness and circularity can be traced to ancient historical and philosophical roots, but more recently the circular economy in particular has been influenced by sprouting schools of thought that include the Cradle to Cradle (C2C) paradigm, the Performance Economy, Biomimicry, Industrial Ecology, Natural Capitalism, Blue Economy, and Regenerative Design. The concept of the embedded economy, in turn, is often traced to Karl Polanyi's (1944) substantivist approach to economic activity and the formalist-substantivist debates that ensued in anthropology and the social sciences. Polanyi argued that market societies (in comparison to preindustrial capitalist societies) rationalize and detach economic activity from social life and its institutions (family and kinship, religion, politics). Granovetter (1985), following suit, argued that even in market economies, economic activity is not as disconnected from society as neoclassical economic models would have it. Economic formalists essentially depict preindustrial economies as yet-to-modernize capitalist economies and humans as rational beings with a universal and eternal desire to maximize profit. Echoing the work of Andreotti (2011a, 2015) and countless others, what this teleological reasoning of human desire forecloses is the possibility that other forms of progress and development exist or are possible.

Neoclassical economic models build on notions of equilibrium and are guided by mechanisms portrayed in terms of "simple linear, causal relationships" (Allen & Boulton, 2011, p. 174). As Allen and Boulton (2011) explain, "any uncertainty or variety of learning or historicity or the possibility of multiple and reflexive inter-relationships are largely ignored with the models" (p. 174). Not only do such models assume closed systems, and a teleological end-goal of equilibrium, they assume "a preordained end point to which things naturally move" (Allen & Boulton, 2011, p. 175). Whether or not we agree with the idea that humans by default act rationally, how to universally frame and define *rationality*, or meaningful measures of profit, in differentiated (cultural, ideological) contexts remains unclear. Marshal Sahlins's (2009) classic theory of the "original affluent society" serves as a potent reminder and possibility, if not evidence-based fact, that value systems are relative and that understandings of profit need not, by definition, be solely measured in accumulation of (tangible) wealth and material goods.

Although access to the profits that health, leisure, social connection, and self-fulfillment provide indeed appear to correlate with material wealth in contemporary societies, their value and our access to them are conditioned by the social arrangements, relations, and systems of meaning we create. Circular and embedded economics have gained momentum as alternatives that disrupt confidence in the linear and enclosed thinking that characterize neoclassical economics. Part and parcel of what many now reference as the solidarity economy (a burgeoning movement to build a just and sustainable economy that has emerged across national and continental contexts), they are redefining the meanings of growth associated with a "take-make-waste" extractive model that prioritizes pro-ductivity and efficiency at all cost. Resituating economic activity within human and nonhuman relations and needs, these alternative economic models allow us to upend and question basic but sanctified assumptions: Productivity and efficiency for whom, toward what end goal, and across which time frame?

A fundamental component of climate change concerns the effects and interconnectedness of economic activity across scope and scale at global, national, and local levels, across time. The fourth U.S. national climate assessment estimates a 10 percent shrinkage in the U.S. economy by the year 2100 due to the adverse effects of environmental degradation (Reidmiller et al., 2018). Students and scholars alike need conceptual frameworks that allow us to not only reimagine and reverse the cause-and-effect trajectory of climate change, but to rethink the validity of, and include in delibera-tions the mounting critiques against, linear infinite growth economics as the only legitimate model of development (Raworth, 2017, D'Alisa et al., 2014, Daly, 1991). As a female front-runner and critic of classical economic thinking, Kate Raworth (2017) has developed an ambitious model that problematizes conventional theory, with its externalization of the adverse effects economics has for sustaining life on earth.

In efforts to balance planetary needs and boundaries with fundamental human social needs (life essentials), Raworth's circular "doughnut economics" attempts to reconcile the outer limits of earth's planetary boundaries (following Rockström et al., 2009) with the inner limits of our social foundation boundaries (following the UN SDG framework). Figures 2.3 and 2.4 below provide visuals of these planetary and human needs and boundaries, alongside their overreach and shortfall (in dark gray, protruding inward and outward from the main circle—or doughnut).

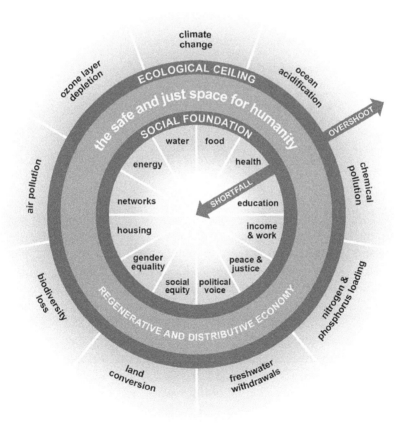

Figure 2.3. Doughnut Economics. *Source*: Kate Raworth, CC-BY-SA-4.0.

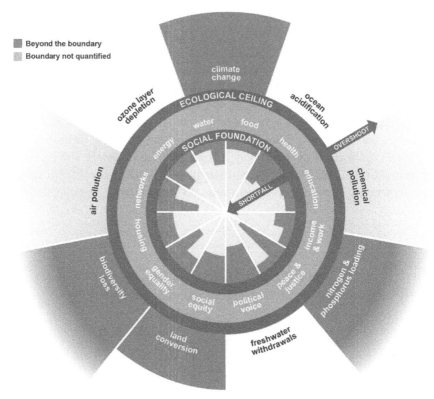

Figure 2.4. Doughnut Economics—Beyond Boundaries. *Source*: Kate Raworth, CC-BY-SA-4.0.

The dark gray perimeters flanking the main circle (doughnut) represent the inner social foundations and outer ecological limits, within which safe and just life on earth exists. A graphic representation of the "world we want," the various dimensions of Raworth's doughnut align with the goals and targets of the SDG framework.

Contemporary research points to consumer society and consumption patterns as central drivers of climate change, with researchers earmarking "consumption as the largest component of aggregate production and economic growth affecting climate change" (Fiske et al., 2018, p. 6). Heeding these findings, and acknowledging that consumption patterns are inherently embedded within sociocultural norms, values, and traditions, we can no longer afford to abstract habits and rules governing consumer societies from the dynamics of climate change. Understanding the global economics of consumption patterns and their effects on the environment require that we situate consumer practices within the particulars of diverse social and cultural contexts. If consumption indeed is a foremost anthropogenic driver of climate change, we need to question how everyday lifestyle choices people make across varied landscapes impact the economics of ecology. How does consumption differ across cultures, and what forces and factors mediate their associated behaviors at the local level?

As part of our study abroad course to Norway during the summer 2022—where we learned about governmental and local native responses to climate change—students were asked to keep a daily "climate journal" in which they catalogued a summation of their consumption, their experiences of the environment, and their feelings about climate change. In analyzing and synthesizing their results, students remarked on the impact that keeping this daily journal had for understanding their own habits, for registering causality they might otherwise have missed if not deliberately tracking their behavior patterns, and for comparing how and why their (estimated) environmental footprint differed between home and abroad, as well as pre- and post-travel. As one student describes,

> Keeping this journal . . . made me think more about climate change, my contributions, and the future. Taking a look at my pre-trip consumption was pretty eye opening after less than a week. I realized early on just how often I was leaving the house to buy coffee or takeout, and it racked up fast. When you're stuck in your routine you don't realize the effects it has, but when you have to take a step back and record your daily actions and consumptions, it makes you aware fast. I noticed early on that every day I was leaving my house and driving about fifteen minutes out to Starbucks, buying an overpriced coffee, and driving home. Once I noticed that, I was like "wow that's ridiculous" and started just making coffee at home again, and was instantly saving a lot of gas and money.

Another student similarly described the changes they went through as the result of exposure, learning, and self-reflection:

> When I first came into the [study abroad] program and was living in New York I had generally formed the idea that what I eat and where I buy it from doesn't really impact the environment. I never considered my electric consumption to be

> something of a big deal . . . it wasn't until [I] logged day in and day out what the climate was like, that I started to notice trends that seemed out of the usual in comparison to previous years.
>   . . . When I got to Norway my resource consumption became so much more conscious . . . [because of] the lessons and speakers . . . [in] the curriculum. The impact it had on me was really big and as a result I took shorter showers, I began to walk more, I didn't buy a fan and I always took note of how I could be better the next day in terms of energy and resource usage.

Building on these and like examples, how might we begin to move toward and envision even deeper shifts in thinking that can mitigate anthropogenic drivers contingent upon lifestyle choices in different consumer societies? What values, needs (perceived or real), and status concerns intrude upon our ability to adjust behavior, in efforts to seek meaningful and fulfilling lives beyond consumer fetishism and a fixation on things material? Decarbonizing the global economy will require a fundamental paradigm shift in thinking vis-à-vis what and how we consume, and in our perceptions of what we need and want. It will require fundamental structural changes that redress unfolding environmental degradation and climate catastrophe, both imminent and long-term, so that we can sustain humanity, life on earth, and our planetary support systems.

As fundamental building blocks of life and the foundation upon which societies organize the production and distribution of resources required for collective sustenance and well-being, economics must integrate into theory and practice the needs and bounds of all human and other-than-human life on earth. If economic efficiency is to accurately account for the net balance between input and output, all costs and benefits must be brought into the fold. This includes the enormous expense of resource depletion and natural systems devastation (Gund Institute for Environment, n.d.). Ecological economics has emerged as a broad, transdisciplinary umbrella term and field of research with focus on the interdependence of human economic activity and the earth's natural ecosystems across space and time (Xepapadeas, 2016). Extending economic theory and calculations beyond conventional focus on built capital (goods and services), ecological economics incorporates human capital (health, education, etc.), social capital (family, friends, community), and natural capital (planetary ecosystems) into analyses.

In order to understand our anthropogenic role amid this multidimensional economic calculus, critical thinking and contemplative criticality is indispensable. It demands that we expand our field of vision and sense of time, and reconsider our wants and desires beyond the realm of immediate perceptibility. It demands opening our habits of thinking and welcoming heterodox, unfamiliar, unsettled, and more convoluted ways of discerning the world, including non-Western economic perspectives that hail from unfamiliar frames of reference. Examples include Buddhist economics, which seeks to contextualize all humans and nature as fundamentally interdependent, and centerstage spiritual values in measures of growth and development (i.e., gross national happiness). Such economic thinking stands in sharp contrast to Western prescripts of gross domestic product (GDP) as a measure of material accumulation (goods and services). Similarly, the *Buen Vivir* movement, with roots in Indigenous practices that have gained ascendancy across Latin America, embrace a holistic and collectivist worldview. The concept of *buen vivir* ("living well") shares principles with other world Indigenous cultures, including *ubuntu* from South Africa, which understands individual human well-being as inseparable from "harmonious relationships with the wider community—including people, the environment, other living beings, their ancestors and the cosmos" (Selibas, 2021, para. 9).

Buen Vivir has kindled increasing mobilization around controversial issues related to land rights, food sovereignty, "environmental justice, economic solidarity and the protection of biodiversity" (Selibas, 2021, para. 9). Such vibrant social organization signal a global awakening surrounding the limitations and narrow worldview of individualism and extractive capitalism. Still evolving and pluralistic in approach, the "good life" philosophy of Buen Vivir represents a decolonial philosophy that strives toward a different paradigm in which the commons is characterized by social, ecological, and cosmic inclusivity (Salazar, 2015, para. 8). Happiness, well-being, and the "good life" is not assessed in logarithmic units of economic measurement, by individual material accumulation, or in relation to brute capitalist production and consumption. It is conceptualized as part of the neologism "sumak kawsay" (*collective* good living): the native Andean notion of living collectively in harmony with other humans, other-than-humans, nature, and the universe.

As a cultural-political project, Buen Vivir does not seek to romanticize the return to an erstwhile ancestral past, but rather to "construct common ancestral futures, where different knowledges come together" and give way to possibilities other than those conscribed by a singular Western rationality prefaced on dominance and hierarchies of belonging (Salazar, 2015, para. 25). Collective visions of the good life, or "good living," rooted in interdependency, is not possible without compassion and collaboration, which necessarily form the beginnings and basis of living in harmony with each other and all life on earth. Conceding to the power of our interdependency, compassion, and collaboration is the "red thread" and connective tissue that runs through otherwise possibilities. It is the through line deactivated by individualistic institutional structures and arrangements that obstruct interdependent sustainable lifeways, the connective tissue that stretches, winds, and tangles but never breaks. It is the subject of chapter 3.

Chapter Three

Compassionate Collaboration

Survival of the Kindest

Contested notions of "truth" notwithstanding, the COVID-19 pandemic undeniably exposed "some ugly truths" (Miranda, 2020, para. 1). They include racial and economic inequities worldwide and, in the United States more specifically, the contours of a "rugged individualism run amok" (Miranda, 2020, paras. 1–6). For those who elevate individual rights far above the greater good, and whose sensibilities are offended when their individual freedoms feel encroached upon, a form of toxic individualism was unleashed amid pandemic battles over mask mandates—with detrimental potential for public health and human life. Nobel Prize laureate Paul Krugman (2020) likened this peculiar American vision of a "good society"—distinguished by its "unrestricted profit maximization . . . and unregulated consumer choice"—and its potentially life-threatening points of contention over masks, to a political ideology of irresponsibility and narcissistic "cult of selfishness" (paras. 6–7).

To cut to the chase, what does contemporary Western (neoliberal) individualism—rooted in patriarchal conquest and competition, white supremacy, myths of manifest destiny, and survival of the fittest—mean for collaborative sustainability and our shared future on earth? A decade ago, Aaron Barlow (2013) traced seemingly intractable cultural and political divides in the United States, which reached a tipping point during the Pandemic, to the "cult of individualism." As an ideology, individualism fetishizes the self as independent of all else and our reliance on each other as social beings, its logic defying our interdependencies on each other and other-than each other (nature, animals, ecosystems). Yet all the while, the environmental challenges confronting human and nonhuman life, more than ever, demand global collaboration and cooperation that crosscut diverse cultural lifeways, varied knowledge orthodoxies, and open-minded inquiry. If we hope to negotiate the intricacies, fluidity, and interconnectivity of a global world, while engaging the place-based drivers that influence climate change in different localities, we will need to work together.

Broadly conceived as a point of departure around which collective cooperation can be conceptualized, this chapter explores evolving fields of expertise and practice that galvanize nodes of interconnection regardless of subject matter or field of study, across scope and scale: at the levels of discipline and academy, local community, regional-national alliances, and global cultural diversity. The (3C) *compassionate collaboration* competency signals the need for global humanity to unite around democratic knowledge production and cooperation in order to advance sustainable pathways. The cartography in figure 3.1 below spotlights the broad contours of compas-

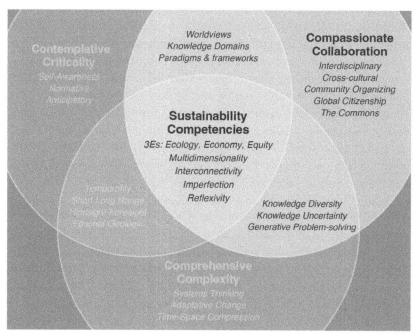

Figure 3.1. 3C Compassionate Collaboration Diagram. *Source*: Created by the author.

sionate collaboration across dimensions: culture, nation-state, community, discipline and industry, and the global commons. At the peripheries are shifting signifiers that intersect and influence collaboration—as an iterative process embedded within human social relations and human relations to the environment: worldviews and knowledge diversity, paradigms and frameworks for understanding life and phenomena, knowledge domains informed by expertise and specialization, and the uncertainty and generative problem-solving that varying perspectives yield.

The chapter explores evolving areas of expertise and education practices that garner hope for cultivating our social interactive and collaborative competency with compassion—as global citizens who must collectively envision and enact sustainable futures together. Using knowledge derived from diverging fields of study, education content must coalesce across disciplinary, cultural, and ideological boundaries, and prepare students to cooperate around competing claims to knowledge. This requires disrupting deeply sedimented orthodoxies (often unconscious) that classify and fragment knowledge and its accumulation throughout education, however. It further requires questioning ubiquitous notions of individualism and separability. Evidence of our inseparability and interconnectedness as a social species continues to accumulate, particularly regarding the key role that compassion and caring play for our survival and wellbeing (Seppälä, 2013). The counterslogan "survival of the kindest" has gained traction as a rebuttal to the lasting legacies and determinism that social Darwinism spawned. It serves to redirect our focus from the inevitability of competition for survival toward compassion, empathy, and care as innate responses increasingly understood as intrinsic to our survival (Seppälä, 2013).

Contrary to the rising tide of evidence, classical economics and sociopolitical structures continue to reinforce individualism and competition as inevitable facts of life, with adverse effects for cooperation and collaboration in ways that can be difficult to pinpoint. Against the backdrop of sweeping neoliberal transformations across sectors of society for example, the obstacles that top-heavy, corporatized education models present for collaboration (rather than competition) in efforts to advance generative knowledge diversity have become legion. As Alvarez (2021) notes, the neoliberal project has "wormed its way into and reshaped our minds and our cultural, political, and economic institutions . . . including universities" (para. 9). It takes for granted assumptions that are far from established, but that have settled into the inner workings of our minds in ways we may be unaware of.

Referencing Cornel West, Alvarez (2021) describes that "the wholesale commodification and bureaucratization of higher education [has made] it difficult to put the focus [on dysfunction] where it belongs" (para. 6). Such observations resonate with earlier arguments advanced in the landmark *Habits of the Heart* (Bellah et al., 1985; 1991), which characterized American individualism as so inscribed with "individualistic achievement and self-fulfillment that . . . it [becomes] difficult for people to sustain their commitments to others, either in intimate relationships or in the public sphere" (p. 425). Yet entrenched individualism stands in diametric contradistinction to understandings of "the individual [as] realized only in and through community" (Bellah et al., 1991. p. 425). This has profound implications for our collaborative resourcefulness. Before addressing fields of study and practice with significance for global cooperation and cross-fertilizing potential, I contextualize the challenges that compassionate collaboration presents within the individualizing constraints of neoliberal restructuring. Over the past half century the "cult of individualism" evolved into a vulgar neoliberal variant, uprooting foundational support structures and social institutions that could otherwise connect us.

Individualism, Neoliberalism, and Collaboration

The ideological intersections between individualism and contemporary neoliberalism are not difficult to trace, with competition, profit, and self-interest as presumed innate motivations driving social relations. Human social dispossession is reduced to individual indolence or ineptitude. *Neoliberalism* is often defined as the resurgence of economic liberalism (free-market capitalism) configured along the trifecta policy prongs of free trade and economic deregulation, privatization of public goods and industries, and austere government spending. Sitaraman (2019) defines the concept along four component parts: deregulation, liberalization, privatization, and austerity (a.k.a. DLPA). In this rendering, liberalization is characterized as the "global counterpart to deregulation" (Sitaraman, 2019, p. 18). Despite its variations in particular locations, the ideology, development model, and policy approach of neoliberalism has succeeded in displacing public goods for private corporations, cooperation for competition, and our sense of commons for the fittest able to survive, around the world (Sitaraman, 2019).

The global hegemonic reach of neoliberal individualism is often traced historically to the economic liberalism and laissez-faire politics that rose to prominence in the eighteenth- and nineteenth-century New World—rooted in the Western Enlightenment philosophies of natural rights and the rights of the individual. In the United States, this version of individualism aggressively promoted private property, ownership, and capital accumulation by dispossession (Harvey, 2004), extolling such traditional "American values" as liberty, personal freedom, and limited government. The renowned nineteenth-century French political scientist Alexis de Tocqueville (2000) described the American democratic tradition as a form of individualism that—when taken to the extreme—encourages "each to their own" mentality and threatens the "virtues of public life": "Individualism is a reflective and peaceable sentiment that disposes each citizen to isolate himself from the mass of those like him and to withdraw to one side with his family and his friends, so that after having thus created a little society for his own use, he willingly abandons society at large to itself" (2000, pp. 482–483).

Individualism creates artificial boundaries that atomize humans from each other and from other-than-human life. It has cataloged groups of people along hierarchies of value, creating tropes of difference that constrain rather than celebrate varied lifeways and our collective vitality. Rarely does the layperson question what individualism actually is and is not, however, or counter its inconsistencies with the ubiquitous interdependencies of life. As Aaron Barlow (2013) makes clear, "everything we do is predicated on interaction with others . . . from language to land use and even to the barriers we create around us" (p. xi). But as the author also reminds us, individualism is "as much a cultural phenomenon as it is a human one" (Barlow, 2013, p. xi). As with all cultural constructs, historical categories that divide and disconnect us not only shift over time, but can be undone (Ignatiev & Garvey, 1996).

The entwined tension between the rights of the individual versus responsibility to the community (collective)—be this local, global, or anywhere in between—thus deserves careful attention and deliberation amid the political crosshairs of neoliberal individualism. When taken to its logical conclusion, neoliberal ideology is the antithesis of things communal, collaborative, or compassionate. It impedes the interpersonal, intercultural, and interdisciplinary capital needed to advance altruistic understanding of global human and nonhuman life and how everyday lived experience contributes to climate change. In short, it has displaced the type of wealth, well-being, and prosperity that materialize when we care for one another and nourish collective belonging through compassion, cooperation, and care.

In his book *The Great Democracy*, Sitaraman (2019) heralds the coming collapse of neoliberal ideology, with its "radical individualism" and failure to provide even near "plausible solutions to today's problems" (p. 56). Instead, its devastating *durée* leaves behind "the complete wreckage of economic, social, and political life" (Sitaraman, 2019, p. 45) amid a world in crisis. Fizzling from relevance, with aimless aspiration for improving our future,

> the neoliberal era offers no serious ideas for how to confront the collapse of the middle class and the spread of widespread economic insecurity. [. . .] no serious ideas for how to address the corruption of politics and the influence of moneyed interests in every aspect of civic life—from news media to education to politics and regulation. [. . .] no serious ideas for how to restitch the fraying social fabric, in which people are increasingly tribal, divided, and disconnected from civic community. [. . .] no serious ideas for how to confront the fusion of oligarchic capitalism and nationalist authoritarianism that has now captured major governments around the world—and that seeks to invade and undermine democracy from within. (Sitaraman, 2019, p. 57)

In order to advance sustainable solutions that transcend the confines of neoliberal market fundamentalism, epistemological hegemony, and culturally prescribed (Western civilizing) worldviews, collaborative learning must widen the purview of problem-solving, integrate pluralistic participatory practices, and harness far more inclusive collective habits of mind. Indeed, scholars caution that traditional approaches to higher education, defined by disciplinary and institutional boundaries, may not adequately prepare students for the complexity and controversy characterizing contemporary global transformations (American Association of Colleges & Universities, 2018).

Venturing beyond the conventional bounds of education content and praxis has proved more and more challenging with the creep of corporatization across higher education, however. More than a decade ago, Nicolaus Mills (2012) lamented the adverse effects of an increasingly corporatized higher-education model, under the tyranny of competitive college and university rankings, the rise of an inflated and increasingly imperious administrative class, and eroding government investment in (public) education. Pre-COVID-19 data revealed a startling state of affairs in the United States: since the 1970s, full-time faculty in higher education had grown 50 percent, in line with increased student enrollment, compared to the 85 percent growth in administrators and 240 percent growth in staff needed to assist administrators (Mills, 2012).

In short, neoliberal corporatization has encroached upon public sector industries that we, as a people, long preserved as our collective rights and responsibilities, including our right to quality public education. The Global Campaign for Education documents the corrosive consequences that chronic underfunding and education privatization have had for education inequality and social segregation (Walker et al., 2016). Little by little, we have witnessed the usurpation of education—private and public—by corporatized logic, its administrative leadership besieged by lawyers and business professionals, often with minimal expertise in the field of education (Ginsberg, 2011). At the granular college campus level, administrative bloat has been traced to increased spending on student services and upscale amenities (i.e., extravagant food courts, glamorous athletic facilities) that cater to student "customers" who demand satisfaction in return for the high cost of tuition in a competitive market. Such spending outpaced investment in academic instruction and tuition subsidies (Mills, 2012), including learning opportunities that allow students and teachers to experiment outside the contours of market efficiency and technocratic conditioning.

Corporatization of higher education has typically prioritized institutional efficiency at the expense of pedagogy and learning, with particular ramifications for socially embodied learning. Despite broad recognition that trained teachers comprise a crucial component of quality education, for instance, their expertise is threatened by cost-effective virtual learning and standardized lessons that rely on reduced human resources and face-to-face social interaction (Walker et al., 2016). In higher education, a net result includes loss of faculty input in decision-making, dwindling tenured and tenure-track positions (from 67 percent in the 1970s to 30 percent in 2012), and the emergence of an academic underclass who—despite being tertiary education's raison d'être—are "on the lowest rung of the academic ladder" (Mills, 2012, para. 17). If we wish to see meaningful change, according to Mills (2012), faculty will need to reclaim the power surrendered to professional administrators over the years, and government(s) will need to reinvest in education, including higher education. More specifically, we will need to invest in models that encourage us to collaborate beyond ivory towers and siloed disciplinary bounds.

The remainder of this chapter explores evolving fields of expertise that serve as building grounds for the pluralistic, cross-fertilizing and multidimensional compassionate collaboration that climate change necessitates, organized under three subheadings: "Collaborative Knowledge and Academic Interdisciplinarity"; "Global Citizenship and Inclusive Democratic Engagement"; and "Contested Knowledge, Conflict Competency, and Compassion." Needless to say, these fields of study and praxis do not comprise an exhaustive tool kit for cultivating collaborative competency. Instead they serve as a starting point for examining the knowledge diversity, democratic participation, civic engagement, intercultural competence, and conflict negotiation needed across academics and the professions, in a diverse multicultural world. The synthesizing thread that runs through collaborative competency across each of these fields is compassion. It is what brings meaning to life and living together.

Collaborative Knowledge and Academic Interdisciplinarity

As a field of study, interdisciplinary scholarship has ebbed and flowed at the margins of academics, and has crystallized into a field with inferior acclaim despite its sought-after acumen. It has evolved into a problem-oriented study that seeks to address social, technical, and policy-related issues, with less focus on discipline-specific depth and academic prowess (Institute for the Study of Science, Technology and Innovation, n.d.). Despite the infamous difficulties noted by scholars devoted to interdisciplinary research and collaboration (institutional, ideological, interpersonal), the strength of interdisciplinarity remains its commitment to learn, critically think, and collaborate across specializations and perspectives. In a global world and workforce characterized by accelerated complexity, uncertainty, and change, ability to master cross-fertilizing and dynamic approaches carries great weight.

Integrating disciplinary perspectives from across the humanities, social sciences, natural sciences, and arts, interdisciplinary studies (IDS) is often touted as facilitating a crowded constellation of learning outcomes: applying the expertise of diverse perspectives as a resource for learning and knowledge production; cultivating effective communication, integrating knowledge through cooperation and collaboration; negotiating interpersonal differences and mediating group conflicts as part of problem-solving; bridging theory to practice and applying curriculum to lived experience and professional expertise; and fostering a sense of social responsibility around contemporary problems at local and global levels. The National Academy of Sciences (2004, p. 2) defines *IDS* as "a mode of research by teams or individuals that integrates information, data, techniques, tools, perspectives, concepts, and/or theories from *two or more* disciplines or bodies of specialized knowledge to advance fundamental understanding or to solve problems whose solutions are beyond the scope of a single discipline or area of research practice."

Upon careful consideration, this definition reveals the omnipresence of interdisciplinarity despite prevailing cultural and institutional barriers—that plural approaches to understanding have always existed as part of comprehensive perspectives. The history of philosophy and learning teaches us that academic disciplines emerged and became increasingly specialized in response to modernity and its evolution. In her latest edition of *The New Education*, Cathy Davidson (2017) explains how the need for a professional-managerial class during the Industrial Era paved the way for higher education's current hierarchical infrastructure, with its disciplinary majors and minors, graduate and professional schools, assessment grades, credits hours, entrance exams, university rankings, philanthropic endowments, and so forth. Increased specialization has in many ways brought disciplines full circle back to interdisciplinarity, with subfield expertise crosscutting disciplinary boundaries in ways that affirm ubiquitous interconnections, regardless of knowledge field. Despite reminders that "everything is now interdisciplinary," however, a great deal of work remains if we are to advance interdisciplinarity to fruition.

Some of the most trenchant challenges to interdisciplinarity within and outside the academy relate to firmly anchored institutional structures that impede cross-sectional collaboration and interactive pedagogies. The tenure-track reward system is often cited as a formidable obstacle that discourages innovative experimentation for fear of failure to keep pace and advance professionally (Pellmar & Eisenberg, 2000). Within the current confines of higher education, interdisciplinary collaboration often goes unrewarded and is risky. It consumes coveted time and energy on the treadmill of productivity and is antagonistic to the competitive thrust of academics as we know it. This is not to denounce tenure and its importance for academic freedom or employment security, but to signal lasting inequities endemic to age-old structures of academic reward and recognition.

As Davidson (2017) argues, the institutions of higher education of today were designed 150 years ago. They date back to the days of Charles

Eliot, eminent president of Harvard University and architect of the American system of research, who in 1869 advocated for radical change in his manifesto "The New Education." The structures put in place at that time have not changed much since, however, despite the drastically different world we now live in. Problematic vestiges of these archaic structures reinforce specialized curricular content that too often fails to translate into the adaptive skills and professional needs of contemporary times. If we are to diversify curricula in ways that reflect student aspirational goals and prepare them for a world in flux, however, faculty will require bona fide recognition, allocated time, and tangible support (resources). It demands that we designate (and honor) time to explore and design new learning content, collaborate across disciplines, experiment with interactive pedagogies, and revamp restrictive assessment measures, to better suit the complexities of our time.

Structural change must penetrate the venerable systems of oversight for tenure and promotion, including ongoing evaluation that place faculty devoted to teaching or institutional service at a disadvantage. Davidson (2023) urges us to reconsider the inverted triangulated pyramid that elevates research as the pinnacle of academic prestige, while teaching and service withers to the bottom. In its place she envisions a square with four mutually reinforcing corners, each accredited with equal value: research, teaching, service (institutional leadership), and "public impact." In this model, the ordinarily excluded but vital role of public engagement is reinserted into the mix. I interpret this to include such notable but typically (formally) unrecognized components as social responsibility, civic engagement, applied (sub)disciplines, advocacy, and activism, among others.

Davidson's quadrangular vision encapsulates the urgent need to reinvest in the publics, and the role of education as a catalyst for cocreating a thriving democratic society that represents all, rather than an elite few. Moreover, her analyses draw attention to longstanding institutional barriers with deep roots in modern-colonial ways of thinking, relating, and arranging that serve to foreclose otherwise possibilities, that undermine imaginaries outside modern-colonial frames of reference (Stein, 2019b). Unable to think beyond the contours of individualism, separability, specialization, universalist knowledge claims, nation-state and ethnic divides, or global capitalist structures, we remain hostage to the fragmented views and machinations that modern-colonial systems impose (Stein, 2019b, p. 669). This begs the question of whether the "master's house" (Lorde, 1984), or the "house that modernity built" (Stein, 2019b), can ever be dismantled using the "master's tools" (Lorde, 1984)?

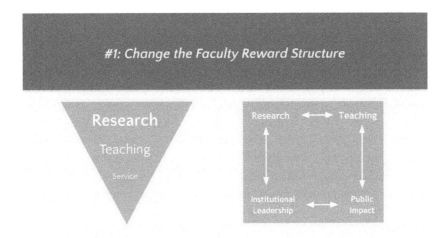

Figure 3.2. Changing the Faculty Reward Structure. *Source*: Davidson (2023, slide 20). Used with permission.

If we are to "liberate humans from the circumstances that enslave them" (Horkheimer, 1982, p. 244), we need to step outside the modern-colonial frameworks that impede alternative possibilities, sense-making, and lifeways from materializing (Stein, 2019, p. 679). By bringing the constraints that limit our view into focus, we can make intelligible previously unimaginable possibilities and maintain hope for alternative lifeways (Stein, 2019b). Making the "previously unimaginable" more intelligible implores us to develop mechanisms for unlearning inherited colonialities that trap us in vested thinking and ordering logics (addressed in chapter 2). This notably includes colonial worldviews and "rights" to land and the environment that continue to do great damage to life on earth. Toward this end, and building on the premise that all curricular subjects throughout academics should, at this historical juncture, invest in alternative sustainable lifeways, education must work to improve pathways for engaging in interdisciplinary collaboration and stepping outside the comfort zones of convention.

Faculty interested in sustainability, moreover, need sufficient resources and support to experiment with course design across programs of study. This has become increasingly difficult considering the austerity of neoliberal restructuring in a post-COVID-19 landscape. More and more, it feels like the weight of the world lands at the doorstep of college—at the feet of faculty who remain the first line of defense for students struggling to reconcile their burgeoning independence, shifting identities, and sense of discombobulation in a turbulent world. The list of privations that encroach on learning and classroom dynamics has grown exceedingly long, and can include anything from vastly varied learning needs or explosive political triggers to overburdened work schedules, primary caretaking responsibilities, mental health challenges, food insecurity, and housing instability. As the *Chronicle of Higher Education* report "On the Verge of Burnout" attests, faculty are "overworked, stressed and thoroughly exhausted" (Tugend, 2020, p. 4). The research conducted for the report revealed high levels of stress, anxiety, and frustration among the professoriate, which was attributed to increased workloads and the "deterioration of work-life balance" (Tugend, 2020, p. 2).

For scholars to invest in cross-fertilizing curricular design and model collaboration as part of inquiry and learning, they will need relief and the institutional conditions that allow them to experiment outside academic divides. Interdisciplinary collaboration organically exposes students to the cooperative capacity upon which complex problem-solving builds, while fostering a sense of collective responsibility. Increasingly, the public and private sectors alike call upon professionals with interdisciplinary expertise and collaborative competency to address the "wicked problems" confronting society. Grohs et al. (2018) cite the National Science Board, Department of Education, National Academy of Engineering, National Institutes of Health, and National Research Council as key among U.S. institutions that praise cross-disciplinary proficiency (p. 110). It is incumbent upon us to ask how we can expect future professionals to collaborate when we have practices in place that hinder collaboration among ourselves. As such, we remain part of the problem rather than the solution.

Education that aims to advance the 3Es of sustainability across disciplines must build on critical and self-reflexive approaches that resist the homogenizing effects of coloniality and ethnocentric epistemology. As the challenges facing us increase in complexity at accelerated rates, boundaries between the natural sciences, social sciences, humanities, and arts continue to serve as barriers that constrain intersecting innovation. Beyond the challenges of advancing interdisciplinarity across academics, moreover, is an even wider chasm between academics and the professions: that "between the well-structured and bounded problems of formal education and the ill-structured nature of work in the professional world" (Grohs et al., 2018, p. 111; see also McNeill et al., 2016; Patil et al., 2015). If we are to prepare students and future global leaders for the heavy lift ahead, the burdens that such theory-practice divides impose must find expression as part of problem-solving. Global citizenship education attempts to bridge the gap between classroom education and the world by connecting what students learn to global civic engagement, a field of study explored in the next section.

Global Citizenship and Inclusive Democratic Engagement

Global citizenship education (GCE) appeals to the needs that accelerated globalization forewarn, and the heightened awareness that civic engagement and cooperation requires recalibrating along global lines. It is characterized as a form of civic learning that focuses on student engagement with social, political, economic, or environmental issues that are increasingly global in scope. In other words, GCE emerged in response to economic and cultural globalization, and the technological advances that have intensified globalization. Descriptions of GCE typically include two mainstay features: global consciousness and global competency. The former involves the range of ethical concerns that shape problems facing us as a common humanity, the latter the skills needed to bring about change and sustainable development in response to the problems we face. As a field of study, GCE seeks to facilitate collaborative learning around globally oriented problem-solving, and builds on central tenets associated with intercultural understanding and tolerance, respect for diversity and inclusivity, civic literacy, human rights and peace, and sustainable development.

As a teaching paradigm, GCE has more recently emerged as a hub of indeterminate activity—scholarship, pedagogy, advocacy, professional training, educational tools—as part of the "internationalization of education." Despite generating a great deal of enthusiasm around its global "transformative" learning aspirations, GCE has received criticism for inadequately theorizing and historicizing its political and philosophical foundations. This is particularly noteworthy in relation to Western educational frameworks for teaching excellence and student learning outcomes (SLOs) that are overdetermined by assessment and metrics as "perverse ends in themselves" (Bamber et al., 2018, p. 205). Scholars further juxtapose two conflicting discourses latent in GCE: one that highlights critical democracy and related ethical values, social responsibility, and civic engagement; the other privileging a market-rationale, self-investment, and economic growth propelled by profits (Pais & Costa, 2020).

Here again we see the recursive imprints of economic liberal and neoliberal structuring, as vestiges of modern-colonial architectures. Because these two conflicting discourses are separate yet not mutually exclusive, they create problematic contradictions. Pais and Costa (2020) argue that critical democratic discourse (à la GCE) has been ineffective in resisting corporatization and commodification, even (particularly) within higher education, which has effectively entrapped academics within complicit and apologetic relations to neoliberal restructuring. Mounting critiques against GCE has led to offshoots that tack "critical" or "transformative" onto global citizenship (i.e., TGCE for transformative global citizenship education), signaling a range of "decolonizing" analyses. These critiques problematize understandings of global citizenship and belonging, and expose the misleading meanings of "global" and "citizen" as (ever) static, singular, uniform, or uncontested.

Critical analyses of GCE challenge implicit hegemonic notions of a "common humanity" that fail to account for economic and cultural inequities (oppression, dispossession) across a complex, volatile global system—distributed along stark North-South divides—and that risk reproducing a new "civilizing mission" (Andreotti, 2011b) with deep roots in Western colonialism. In such a reproductive "civilizing" rendition of globalization, to be "global" is to have enough means to relocate—for purposes of residency or leisure—to another geographic place or through space (as the COVID-19 pandemic made crystal clear, access to virtual technology is far from universal), absent local, national, and international restraints (Shiva, 1998). In the words of Bauman (1998), "the walls of immigration controls, of residence laws and of 'clean streets' and 'zero tolerance' grow taller" if you are not "global" (p. 89). In other words, who the "global citizenry" represents or benefits, as part of GCE discourse, is far from reconciled.

Critiques notwithstanding, a great deal of promising curricula exists under the rubric of global citizenship, to which students should be exposed despite the homogenizing tendencies noted above (Bamber et al., 2018). Twenty-first-century students, as global citizens, must learn to articulate how contemporary global problems are mediated by particular geographic, demographic, and sociopolitical forces, and must acquire the broad knowledge and key competencies required to envision, build, and participate in sustainable futures. In order to cultivate social conscientiousness that resonates in the lives of students, however, curricular content and activities must remain relevant to their experiences, aspirations, and needs as members of their local, variegated communities. Sustainable education must inevitably move from intangible goals at an abstract global level to action that involves human subjectivity and agency at the everyday personal, community, and institutional levels.

We need to build on dynamic educational approaches, models, and tools that move beyond talking points about "transformative change," and empower students to envision concrete action with relevancy for their lives. This resonates with Lisa Patel's (2014) insight, following Tuck and Yang (2012), that "keeping relationships among [human] beings and land abstract and vague" (p. 359) reinforces erasure of harmful mechanisms and their historical roots. How do we render convoluted, interlocking relations, obfuscated from view, more tangible to students around the globe, so that they can envision and act on change? Heeding the expertise and lifeways of local stakeholders and native views of knowledge is a fundamental starting point. Sometimes we fail to see what is right in front of us. Hidden in plain sight, we cannot see because we presume to already know or to know better. In *Pollution Is Colonialism*, Max Liboiron (2021) explains that colonialism is tricky and "lurks in assumptions and premises," even when we are trying to do good (p. 45).

Liboiron captures the absurdity of science detached from human experience and local knowledge in a tale about academic peer review in which "a single knowledge becomes the touchstone for all other knowledge systems" (2021, p. 54). As part of the publication review process for an academic paper on fish, one peer reviewer requests proof of how the authors know the fish was cod. "Because the fishers said so" the scholars quip to each other, laughing. On the island of Newfoundland, cod is integral to the "culture, heritage, diets, livelihoods, songs, and life. . . . Babies know what cod is!" (Liboiron, 2021, p. 55). In order to ensure publication however, the authors must assure the reviewer that a lab member with scientific training witnessed the fish firsthand. The scientific proof is accepted and the paper published. The lab members laugh when acknowledging that the lab "scientist" in question "couldn't tell a goldfish from a mackerel" (Liboiron, 2021, p. 55).

As someone who grew up gutting fish off the side of a boat in the fjords of Norway's west coast during summertime, I recognize the visceral expressions of wisdom that repetitive exposure and muscle memory confer, despite the absence of systematic documentation. The comical symbolism of distinguishing goldfish from mackerel runs deep and becomes somatic. How do we transpose such ingrained knowledge, or even the awareness that we are beholden to such knowledge, into legitimate and applicable expertise? It relates to the version of knowledge that Robin Kimmerer (2013) explores in *Braiding Sweetgrass*, which listens carefully to the language of plants and animals, in addition to humans, and which celebrates our intertwined relationships to all life on earth. In chapter 4, I explore the work of post-normal science and scholars who seek to democratize the scientific knowledge we deem legitimate. A field of study that builds on interdisciplinarity of all kinds, post-normal science attempts to expand the expert community and qualifying "facts" that form the basis of accepted knowledge. It endeavors to broaden the range of stakeholders included in the framing, problem-solving, and assessment processes of knowledge acquisition. In so doing, it expands our fields of vision, accommodates plurality of perspectives, and welcomes value dissent (Kønig et al., 2017).

Efforts to democratize scientific processes are similarly reflected in citizen science initiatives that build on participatory problem-solving and innovation around societal needs. Touted as a means to draw the public into democratic governance, citizen science provides opportunity to participate in the dwindling art of civic engagement. As public scientists who strive to collectively address social problems, participants can use what they learn to influence public policy at various levels. This is vital during a time when faith in democratic governance and civic engagement appears to be at all-time lows. Writing for the *Atlantic* series "Is Democracy Dying?," Appelbaum (2018) describes democratic behavior as a habit that has faded in recent U.S. history. Public trust in government has retracted, alongside participation in civic life. For Appelbaum the solution is practice: democratic behavior is acquired, and "develops slowly over time, through constant repetition" (2018, p. 75).

The decline of civics education in primary and secondary schooling—or all tiers of education—demands that we refocus our attention on the central question of "how we want to live together" (Hess & McAvoy, 2015). But doing so involves more than behavioral repetition and honing our habits. The "signs of underlying decay" in U.S. governance—across structures, systems, and public confidence—owes much of its discontent to the politics of representation (Appelbaum, 2018, p. 75). If representative democracy is to reflect the collective needs and interests of all people, then politics and policies, public narrative, and the popular imagination must resonate with more than privileged groups of people. Students must be initiated in reflection and self-assessment, including collective and institutional self-reflection on behalf of the organizations and communities to which they belong. They must be encouraged to critically (re)examine the histories and definitions of master concepts that guide thinking from early on (i.e., development, progress, modernization, democracy, globalization, sustainability), alongside the social arrangements they take for granted but that fundamentally structure their lives.

Appelbaum (2018) concludes that developing democratic participatory habits of mind must do more than append sundry civics lessons to the already overburdened responsibilities that students confront (p. 77). They amount to more than what we can internalize from textbooks or from perfunctory performance. Cultivating democratic participation involves endowing students with ongoing opportunities, in whatever form or fashion, to "write charters, elect officers, and work through the messy, frustrating process of self-governance" (Appelbaum, 2018, p. 77). These are not to be supplemental activities; they must be center stage of a "basic curriculum of democracy" that is intentional, prioritized, and infused throughout learning (Appelbaum, 2018, p. 77). Time and resource commitments resurface as the critical missing mass that will enable students of any age to collectively identify common goals and action pathways, with the ultimate goal of fostering our global civic responsibility to live together, sustainably. Such prioritization of resources flies in the face of neoliberal efficiency, however, which pushed "democratic governance into retreat" in the first place (Appelbaum, 2018, p. 77).

In 2012, the AAC&U publication *A Crucible Moment: College Learning and Democracy's Future* reported that opportunities for students to expand their civic knowledge and skills had improved over the preceding decades, but that civic learning and democratic engagement needs to become more "pervasive, integrative, and intentional" (National Task Force on Civic Learning and Democratic Engagement [NTCLDE], 2012, p. 3). The report advanced three main strategies for making civic learning and democratic engagement more widely accessible to college students, the first of which includes broadening a "narrowly conceived and outdated definition of what civic learning actually entails" (NTCLDE, 2012, p. 4). Following D. Hoffman's (2015) model of best civic learning and democratic engagement efforts, civics curriculum should (1) be integrated throughout learning and courses, (2) move beyond abstract learning and enable students to establish meaningful relations based in respect for their differences, (3) build on organic opportunities to envision and create new pathways for change, and (4) remain generative of and continually seek to improve the conditions and relationships that enable collective action.

Civic engagement in the digital age provides immense opportunities beyond exercising the right to vote at a ballot box or participating in face-to-face community meetings (as important as these are). Students need authentic, unscripted means of exploring and practicing their evolving democratic sensibilities and collective agency, based in learning experiences that have genuine relevance to their lives. Sustainability curricula will require rebranding the concept of "civics" (including "new civics"), and to examine how its associated meanings can be reconceptualized in order to transcend outdated archetypes and old-guard politics, in forging new pathways for democratic participation that are global in reach. The AAC&U's "Framework for Twenty-First-Century Civic Learning and Democratic Engagement" provides an important template and point of departure that combines four broad learning categories as guideposts: knowledge, skills, values, and collective actions (NTCLDE, 2012, p. 4).

A Framework for Twenty-First-Century Civic Learning and Democratic Engagement

Knowledge	Skills	Collective Action
• Familiarity with key democratic texts and universal democratic principles, and with selected debates—in US and other societies—concerning their applications	• Critical inquiry, analysis, and reasoning	• Integration of knowledge, skills, and examined values to inform actions taken in concert with other people
	• Quantitative reasoning	• Moral discernment and behavior
	• Gathering and evaluating multiple sources of evidence	• Navigation of political systems and processes, both formal and informal
• Historical and sociological understanding of several democratic movements, both US and abroad	• Seeking, engaging, and being informed by multiple perspectives	• Public problem solving with diverse partners
• Understanding one's sources of identity and their influence on civic values, assumptions, and responsibilities to a wider public	• Written, oral, and multi-media communication	• Compromise, civility, and mutual respect
	• Deliberation and bridge building across differences	
	• Collaborative decision making	
• Knowledge of the diverse cultures, histories, values, and contestations that have shaped US and other world societies	• Ability to communicate in multiple languages	
	Values	
• Exposure to multiple religious traditions and to alternative views about the relation between religion and government	• Respect for freedom and human dignity	
	• Empathy	
	• Open-mindedness	
• Knowledge of the political systems that frame constitutional democracies and of political levers for influencing change	• Tolerance	
	• Justice	
	• Equality	
	• Ethical integrity	
	• Responsibility to a larger good	

Figure 3.3. AAC&U Framework for Twenty-First-Century Civic Learning and Democratic Engagement. *Source*: National Task Force on Civic Learning and Democratic Engagement (2012).

An overarching question remains how rapid and increasingly ephemeral changes related to technology are reshaping the ways we conceptualize and engage in democratic participation. One important potential for digital civics is to establish structured virtual opportunities where students with diverse backgrounds, political persuasions, and worldviews can come together to discuss controversial topics with cutting edge currency. Several colleges (CSU Chico, Tarleton State University, Shenandoah University) have begun experimenting with public sphere pedagogy (PSP) and town hall educational programs that bring students and faculty from across disciplines together with community representatives to debate and develop action plans related to important contemporary issues (immigration, racial inequality, etc.). Participating courses integrate scaffolded research and writing on a designated topic in preparation for cross-disciplinary town hall debates where students discuss different perspectives and present action plans. Students are subsequently guided to incorporate feedback received during debate and from faculty in revising their action plans, after the town hall meeting.

Adapting town hall meetings like these to virtual formats provide a potential means of extending the reach of global education to students who cannot participate in study abroad programs. Although the learning that comes with immersive travel experiences in faraway locations is difficult to emulate, online global learning networks like Collaborative Online International Learning (COIL) connect students and faculty in diverse countries and provide access to intercultural exchange. Using existing teaching strategies that mimic town hall meetings (i.e., the Town Hall Circle developed by Facing History & Ourselves) students and faculty can explore topics online from varying national and cultural perspectives. Ideally, the charge to make global education equitable for all would allow students near and far the chance to immerse themselves in distant lifeways that destabilize the familiar, but in lieu of on-the-ground global education exposure, online intercultural collaboration and discussion around thematic issues can build intercultural knowledge into learning.

Virtual intercultural collaboration and learning would allow more students and faculty to explore divergent understandings and perceptions of global problems across differentiated landscapes. Study abroad students could participate in online forums to share their experiences of intercultural learning with a wider audience (i.e., students unable to travel abroad), field questions, and engage in discussion around specified topics. In reviewing student feedback and commentary from our study abroad course in Norway during the summer of 2022 (climate change in cross-cultural perspective), for instance, a common theme that emerged was a shifting sense of hope and possibility for the future. As one student explained,

> before our trip, I didn't really realize I had a pretty nihilistic view of the future. . . . it's not hard to fall into a pattern of negative thinking. I had become one of those people who thought their impact didn't matter, I was wasteful and in a hole. Going abroad and seeing societies where almost everyone and the government take climate change seriously was super helpful. I feel more hopeful for the future now, and I definitely saw that reflected in my journal entries.

Such feedback and reflection could form the basis of broader discussion and cross-fertilization through which students from various cultures exchange and are exposed to differing experiences.

In sum, global citizenship and sustainability education must integrate cross-cultural and cross-disciplinary perspectives, expertise, and best practices in order to assist students in (a) articulating local issues with relevance to their lived experiences and (b) distinguishing the local-to-global-level linkages that characterize contemporary problems affecting them. Related curricula can be structured around existing global civics and interdisciplinary learning outcomes: combining disciplinary perspectives to solve local- and global-level sustainability problems related to course themes (i.e., local food and global systems); facilitating proactive student reflection on their responsibilities as members of their local, regional, and global communities, and their role as agents of social change; bridging theory to practice by connecting academic learning to students' lives on campus, in their local home communities, and in their professional work settings; and encouraging cooperation across differences and competing needs, using ethical and evidence-based reasoning to devise actionable strategies for social change and intervention.

Global education for sustainable development must be grounded in place-based community and human relations that connect diverse knowledge production and historical perspectives to global systems and forces. Using local college community and campus resources, curricula can guide students in identifying grassroots needs that, in turn, are linked to global systems and forces (i.e. food choices, food waste, and food insecurity on campus). Alternatively, broad systemwide drivers can be traced to local-level environmental issues that students, as experts of their own personal, social, and occupational lives, engage through dynamic learning modalities. Sustainability curricula across formal and informal education will in this way be better positioned to connect local-global forms of knowledge to the "wicked problems" we face (Rittel & Webber, 1973), as well as connect disciplinary expertise to sustainable development goals (SDGs) that, in turn, map onto broader, systems-level drivers of climate change.

Worldwide cultural-historical perspectives portend vastly different frameworks for understanding, however. They require that we navigate conflicting foundations of knowledge and contested pathways toward their production. It is through discourse, doubt, disagreement, and dialectical exchange that knowledge remains vibrant and advances. If knowledge is inherently collaborative in this manner, it stands to reason that it will also be contested and conflicted. As such, we need to become more nuanced experts at disagreeing, doubting, and debating across differences. The final section of this chapter explores the productive possibilities of conflict and the importance of harnessing its potential with compassion as part of collaboration.

Contested Knowledge, Conflict Competency, and Compassion

Understandings of knowledge accumulation as dialectically generated are inherently invested in plural perspectives and heterogeneous interpretation. This opens the floodgates to conflicts of interest as situated within the contingencies of sociocultural, political, economic, religious, and historical specificity. Dialectical learning and inclusive knowledge acquisition place considerable burden on our ability to negotiate differences of perception, sentiment, and worldview, and to manage competing claims, as well as on our ability to productively engage conflicts that breathe life into new, generative ways of seeing, sensing, and knowing. Yet in many cultures or communities, conflict avoidance is widespread. Ashkenas (2010) notes that in the corporate world, conflict *avoidance* "is one of the most common characteristics," despite being "one of the most pernicious and danger-ous sources of unintentional complexity" (para. 1). Conflict avoidance is common as part of both routine workplace interaction and strategic decision-making (Ashkenas, 2010).

Prominent motivational figure Brendon Burchard is known for his quote "avoidance is the best short-term strategy to escape conflict, and the best long-term strategy to ensure suffering." The idea of conflict as a productive asset to be nurtured and cultivated can be traced to criminologist and peace scholar Nils Christie's landmark article "Conflicts as Property" (1977). At the heart of Christie's iconoclastic observations was his insistence that conflict is central to all life, that conflict ought not be expropriated by official proceedings that disempower those implicated in its creative capacity. For conflict negotiation to bear the full fruits of its potential, conflicts must be allowed to emerge in their own right. Enabling the conditions that allow conflicts to "flourish and reveal [their] gift" (Barter, 2009) requires interrupting institutional practices that typically contain them. For conflict mediator and dialogical systems designer Dominic Barter (2009), the issue is not simply how to resolve conflicts, but how to have them—allow them to materialize—in the first place. Based on years of professional experience, he explains the importance of creating spaces

> where people [could] bring their conflict so they could have a good fight. So the fight could flourish, fully . . . And when we [circle participants] came to that [restorative] circle, we came to the conflict not with any kind of idea that there was anything wrong with the conflict or there was a problem, something that had to be resolved or made to go away or something needed to be changed. But actually this was an experience of having conflict and people experience that as an opportunity to get powerful and to start working out how to express that power and influence change. . . . It makes a big difference when I think, "Here's a problem that needs to be made to go away" [instead of thinking] "People come together looking for a space where they can fully experience conflict and where it can flourish and reveal its gift to us."

An eminent international restorative circles practitioner whose particular restorative justice brand first gained ascendancy in Brazil, Barter complicates the common conceptions we attribute to conflict. Influenced by restorative justice (RJ) praxis, his signature circle conferencing was developed as an "integrated, systemic response" (Barter, 2012, p. 21) to conflict by providing a unique structure and process that guides difficult dialogue. For Barter (2012), the circle represents one of the "most ancient of social patterns" organized around a foremost premise: "an intention— to recognize the other, to share meaning, to invite truth-telling" (p. 21). The conferencing circle at the core of restorative justice and its offshoots have deep roots in Indigenous practice and tribal justice in various world locations. Compared to Western adversarial systems of justice—where emphasis is on retribution and punishment—Indigenous philosophies focus on addressing discord by teasing out underlying conflicts (the vagaries of norms, values, expectations, and their violations), navigating discrepancies of perception, and repairing harm inflicted on affected individuals and the community (Mallon, 2013). A chief goal of this system is reintegrating members cast out from the community for wrongdoing.

A distinctive feature of restorative approaches thus relates to how we perceive conflict and *who* "we see as being in conflict" (Barter, 2012, p. 70). Restorative conflict intervention moves beyond a dichotomous stronghold that juxtaposes (two) opposing adversaries and marshal members from the wider community of both parties in conflict intervention. "Our formal and informal justice systems seek to define who has done wrong," explains Barter. "However, from the very first experiments involving Restorative Circles with favela youth, it was clear that there were three—not two—parties playing key roles in . . . conflict" (Barter 2012, p. 70). The "conflict community" is responsible for contributing to the conditions within which conflicts occur. Restorative Circles hence recognize a "plurality of victimhood" among conflict participants (Barter 2012, p. 70). Plurality of victimhood captures the multifarious experiences that typically characterize conflicts. It further allows us to honor the contradictions of being "offender" and "victim" at one and the same time, that the "wrongdoers" themselves often share feelings of being wronged in a broader context.

Restorative justice is but one of many approaches to conflict intervention and intercultural dialogue, albeit one that has gained international notoriety over the years. In part, it has come to symbolize a social movement to bring about constructive social change within institutional settings where conflict is rife—courts, prisons, schools, and so forth—but its efficacy is lauded in more informal settings as well. A great deal of literature has accumulated on the history and varieties of restorative justice cross-culturally, including transitional and transformative justice initiatives that extend beyond criminal justice and law and that seek to redress the trauma of historic crimes against humanity (Johnstone & Van Ness, 2013; McEvoy, 2007; Menkel-Meadow, 2007; Nocella, 2011). In other words, many versions of restorative practice(s) exist—including truth and reconciliation commissions (TRCs) or truth, racial healing, and transformation (TRHT) commissions, that aim to reconcile historic harm[1]—in efforts "to make possible more sustainable responses to painful conflict" by convening "those impacted and creating a space where their voices may be heard" (Lyubansky & Barter, 2011, p. 39).

There is a great deal of overlap between restorative, reconciliatory frameworks, and longstanding peace dialogue and conflict mediation models. Notable examples include Marshall Rosenberg's (2003) nonviolent communication (NVC) based on empathy, compassion, and fundamental human needs, and intergroup dialogue (common across college campuses), which similarly builds on face-to-face exchange, empathy, and understanding between different social or cultural groups. The positive conflict transformation approach advanced by John Lederach, in turn, has championed the need for a "sense of belonging" to be inclusive of all stakeholders. As an interdisciplinary field of expertise, peace studies generally recognizes conflict as integral to human social interaction and our collective existence, and seeks to harness adversarial dynamics as a means to bring about transformative change.

Thus, first and foremost, conflict should be channeled for its positive and productive potential. As an offshoot of the Thomas-Kilmann conflict mode instrument (TKI), Carol Wilson's (2014) conflict continuum visual clearly captures the contrast between healthy and unhealthy conflict along a spectrum (p. 268). Sandwiched between the generative attributes that trust encourages at one extreme and the stifling attributes that fear inspires at the other, the conflict continuum charts ingredient criteria that influence the climate within which conflict is embedded.

Figure 3.4. The Conflict Continuum. *Source*: Carol Wilson, personal website, n.d. Used with permission.

Healthy conflict is enabled in an atmosphere where trust and transparency predominates over fear, where people feel safe to speak their mind and can be their true selves. Unhealthy conflict, by contrast, is encouraged in an atmosphere overshadowed by fear, distrust, and humiliation.

No matter what the particular school of thought, constructive approaches to conflict must find their rightful place among the compassionate collaborative competencies that global sustainability necessitates. Young students and lifelong learners need opportunities to practice and hone interpersonal, social, intercultural, and emotional intelligence—at work or in leisure, through conflict and pleasure—as part of the vast but valuable differences that configure diverse geographic and diasporic civilizations worldwide. Compassionate collaboration must heed the multicultural, deliberative forms of reasoning and knowledge accumulation that global diversity embodies. Yet knowledge diversity, with the varied foundations upon which it builds, is a moving target that continually adapts with the passing of time in response to infinite factors, some known and anticipated, others unexpected or ill-defined. This makes for volatile terrain in our efforts to envision alternative futures and few (if any) clear roadmaps for navigating the enormous challenges confronting students and educators alike (Stein, 2018b).

The uncertainty that such dynamic variability and complex causality provoke demand a degree of comfort with the unpredictable and unknown—no matter what the historical and cultural particulars—but also the capacity to think through causality and vectors of climate change in their dynamic, adaptive relations. In the next chapter, I explore our need to cope with such complicated and ambiguous contingencies that are out of our control. Chapter 4 returns to the importance of historical reflexivity and intercultural exchange for understanding the world we inhabit together and analyzing the "wicked problems" we face from a comprehensive, interactive systems perspective. Amid global volatility, uncertainty, complexity, and ambiguity (VUCA), the "wicked problems" that climate change presage warrant integrated analyses of the manifold, interacting, and adaptive forces at play, along socioeconomic, political, cultural, and ecological axes. As a pathway toward the collective global goals of sustainability, we need to better understand the ways in which problems comprise more than the sum of their constituent parts.

Chapter Four

Comprehensive Complexity

Systems, Uncertainty, and Not Knowing

Because so many of the social problems we face are anchored in complex shifting conditions, rapid change, unpredictability in governance, and eroded trust in truth and reason, solutions will require adaptive modes of inquiry that accommodate the intricacies, fluidity, and interconnectivity of the global twenty-first century. Stein (2018b) persuasively argues against "any single arsenal of educational tools—including liberal critical approaches—[that] can adequately equip us to respond generatively, strategically, and ethically to the complex local and global challenges that we currently face" (p. 1). As noted in my introductory chapter, the 3C social cartography is intended as an interactive and shifting conceptual heuristic device that can accommodate an expansive and expanding arsenal of educational tools (approaches, perspectives, models, methods, and so forth). Extending on the limitations of education explored in chapter 3 (circumscribed disciplinary and institutional boundaries), this chapter examines the need for students, scholars, scientists, and practitioners to transgress static, singular, and compartmentalized configurations of learning writ large, so that they are better positioned to tackle the challenges characterizing contemporary global transformations (AAC&U, 2018).

If we are to make sense of the accelerating complexity and volatility surrounding us, we will need to extend systems thinking, become more comfortable with ambiguity, contradiction, and uncertainty, and resign ourselves to the unlikelihood that solutions will be swift, or even exist at all. How might systems thinking help people seek sustainable change amid the vexing challenges confronting us? David Stroh (2015) identifies a series of generative mechanisms that collaborative systems thinking instigate toward this end: it enables people to recognize the ways they exacerbate problems; it exposes people to collectively unsatisfactory results, reinforcing the need to collaborate; it discourages people from trying to do too much with too little, achieving less than what is optimal or possible; and perhaps most important of all, it "forces people to accept that knowledge is never complete or static" (Stroh, 2015, p. 22).

The decisions we make or do not make, now more than ever, have consequences that play out along temporalities and beyond fixed, isolated locations. The time has long since passed for us to redirect focus toward the intertemporal dimensions of our behaviors and actions, as embedded within world geographies that are not (and never where) dispersed and disaggregated. David Harvey's (1990) decades-old notion of time-space compression articulates the altered relationship between, and our adjusted sense of, time and space as technological advance and global interconnection accelerates. In short, our decisions have far-reaching consequences for the present, the future, and the past (how we reconcile, memorialize, and honor ancestry and the worlds we inherit) in global settings near and far as part of our "moving interconnectedness" (Hannerz, 1992). The comprehensive complexity competency of the 3C cartography draws attention to the overlapping and interconnecting intricacies along these multidimensional complexities, in an effort to forge pathways toward sustainable futures.

Figure 4.1 on the opposite page illustrates the key ingredients of complexity explored in this 3C cartography, across intersecting dimensions of time, space, locality (culture), adaptation, and change. At the intersections between comprehensive complexity and its adjacent sustainability competencies (critical contemplation, compassionate collaboration) are infinite inflection points for expanding our understanding: between the knowledge diversity and generative problem-solving competencies that diverging worldviews, wisdom, and practices promise on the one hand, and the depth of insight that intertemporal appreciation provides across scope and scale on the other—whether hindsight (short or long range, epochal), foresight, or the present.

At the core of comprehensive complexity is our ability to understand, but also withstand, how different systems (cultural, political, ecological, etc.) interrelate and adapt through time, space, and physicality, creating enormous unpredictability and uncertainty. The ensuing sections explore

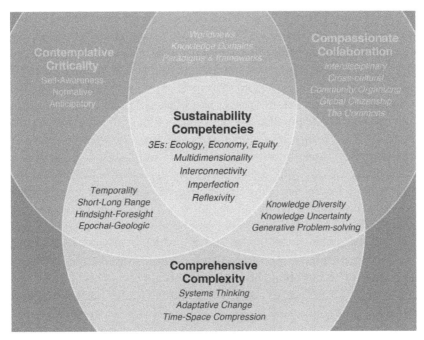

Figure 4.1. 3C Comprehensive Complexity Diagram. *Source*: Created by the author.

these sustainability competencies with emphasis on metacognition and how to manage complexity, ambiguity, and dynamic change, alongside their application within the context of real-world constraints. Moving through the infamous VUCA vocabularies (volatility, uncertainty, complexity, ambiguity), I examine the significance of uncertainty and not knowing—of the known unknowns but also the unknown unknowns (Luft & Ingham, 1955)—and nurturing an ontology of uncertainty that brings metacognitive reflexivity competencies into the fold. The chapter concludes by problematizing tropes of "excellence," and the difficulties that uncertainty and unpredictable experimentation present when failure and the right to be wrong are discouraged or foreclosed.

Complex Adaptive Systems and Systems Thinking Competency

In the early 1990s critical thinking scholar Richard Paul noted that addressing problems of the world involves understanding "corporate, national, trans-national, cultural, religious, economic, and environmental [forces], all intricately intertwined" (1993, p. 13). Recognizing the increasing complexity and ambiguity that accompany social and ecological issues, the sweep of these diverse but intertwined fields point to far more ambitious problem-solving strategies than most are accustomed to. In fact, as Camillus (2008) implies in "Strategy as a Wicked Problem," the concept of strategy may be *the* problem. As the author cautions, many issues cannot be resolved by "gathering additional data, defining [them] more clearly, or breaking them down into small problems" (Camillus, 2008, p. 2). This is particularly the case with wicked problems impervious to lockstep resolve that instead require flexibility in "framing, reasoning and acting within multiple dimensions" (Grohs et al., 2018, p. 111). Wicked problems are characterized by intertwined complexities and unique particularities that typically lack singular solutions, and for which a given solution often involves compromise. At the base level, addressing wicked problems implicate frame reflection and uncertain causality.

The lack of direct or clear, visible causality—often accompanied by extended time frames and levels of remove between an intervention and its impact (Rittel & Webber, 1973)—is in part what renders elucidation of wicked problems difficult. In many respects, wicked problems emulate life itself; they are the meat of the matter that social scientists spend their time ruminating on, often with no more than tentative resolve. Among the primary reasons for their intransigence are difficulties associated with definition and a propensity toward "elusive political judgment for resolution" (Rittel & Webber, 1973, p. 160). In fact, difficulties of definition are considered a foremost ingredient of their intractability: understanding the difference between what we (can) observe and possible (desired) end-goals relies on a host of factors that are subjective by nature, including framing, perspective, approach, context, scope, scale, and so forth.

Grohs et al. (2018), following Rittel and Webber (1973), define wicked problems as "characterized by (a) the unique nature of each problem; (b) the interplay between attempts to address the problem and how it is framed; and (c) the ambiguity of causality, particularly as it relates to the temporal distance between an intervention and any direct effects" (p. 111). The authors argue that wrestling with wicked problems requires not only fluency in critical reasoning, but flexible metacognition that can accommodate responses and attention to framing along multiple interacting dimensions (Grohs et al., 2018). Building on multidimensional cognitive and metacognitive strategies, the authors developed a systems thinking framework that shifts paradigm thinking away from right-wrong reasoning when addressing complex, interdependent, and adaptive problems (Grohs et al., 2018).

For many, reference to "systems thinking" signals the hard sciences and is relegated to the "other side" of a soft-hard science divide. This despite its equal import for understanding phenomena at the crossroads of social science and the humanities, and the subdivisional interdependencies that link sociocultural problems throughout subject matter (Checkland, 1981). Organized around three overarching, intertwined dimensions—problem, perspective, and time—the systems thinking framework developed by Grohs et al. (2018) reveals considerable overlap with the sustainability competencies mapped in this cartography. Following Jonassen (2000) and Paul (1993), the authors describe the first of these—"problem"—as the difference between an existing reality and desired goal (Grohs et al., 2018). Solving problems, by extension, involves a retroductive process of cognition and action with focus on relevant activities for achieving a desired goal. Among them are defining a current versus desired state, identifying existing and needed resources (material and otherwise), identifying stakeholders and their needs, identifying obstacles, and discerning biases and assumptions that influence reasoning (Grohs et al., 2018, p. 112).

Discerning biases and assumptions are particularly relevant in relation to the "naming and framing" (Grohs et al., 2018) of problems, since decisions regarding which conceptual elements to include or exclude in their deliberation are inherently cultural and contextually contingent. The "problem" dimension corresponds with all three competencies around which the 3C cartography is organized (critical contemplation, compassionate collaboration, comprehensive complexity), drawing into orbit any number or range of auxiliary signifiers that emerge at their interstices (i.e., worldviews, paradigms, and knowledge domains; intercultural diversity and knowledge variance; temporality and framing). From an adaptive systems perspective, the "problem" dimension seeks to contemplate the complexities of climate change using intersectional approaches that integrate social, political, economic, cultural, and ecological dynamics across multiscale levels, from "the grain of sand on the beach" to "the planet as a whole" (Eriksen, 2016, p. 28).

Differing worldviews widen or narrow the bounds within which problems are conceptualized and the related scope of problem deliberations. Grohs et al. (2018) identify both the technical (expertise, tools, methods, processes, etc.) and contextual (social, political, economic, legal, ecological, etc.) elements implicated in problem-solving as important, but emphasize their *intertwined* nature as problems increase in complexity. This entangled interconnectedness, as problems increase in complexity, substantiates the need to move beyond models that elevate the hard over soft sciences (or vice versa), and to better synthesize how knowledge variance and their variables interlock. This, in turn, will facilitate and bolster forms of knowledge accumulation that include "voices and perspectives that may be absent, ignored, or suppressed unless specifically identified as a priority" (Grohs et al., 2018, p. 112).

For obvious reasons, absent, ignored, or suppressed voices are especially significant for the "perspective" dimension of a systems thinking framework. This dimension recognizes that the differing values, beliefs, and experiences that stakeholders bring to a problem directly influence how problems are understood and addressed. Framing resurfaces as a central aspect of the challenges involved in tackling socially complex problems, and is defined as the "underlying structures of belief, perception and appreciation" (Schön & Rein, 1994, as quoted in Grohs et al., 2018, p. 113). As with the "problem" dimension, these underlying structures of perspective correspond directly with central components of the 3C cartography, in particular critical contemplation and compassionate collaboration. Self-reflexive and normative competence regarding our own versus other worldviews, paradigms, and forms of knowledge have direct bearing on how we interpret, intercept, and cope with problems.

It comes as no surprise that interventions that seek to redress wicked problems are often stymied by political positioning, stakeholder posturing, and mental constructs that escape reflexive rigor (Grohs et al., 2018). In other words, mental constructs that enter the realm of unconscious assumptions and that are thereby eclipsed from interrogative reasoning. A great deal of problem-solving, policy planning, and decision-making is embedded in and scripted from the cultural assumptions we take for granted and that give meaning to our world, but that all the while subscribe to inherently biased rationalities we may be unaware of. Because no singular (universal) narrative has a premium on "reality," it follows that differing worldviews in which reasoning is necessarily embedded may be in conflict. For this reason, Grohs et al. (2018) articulate the need for participants in policy and planning deliberations to reflect on how problems are framed (and reframed) with intentionality, both individually and collectively—a recommendation that corresponds with both the 3C self-awareness and collective normative competencies.

Grohs et al.'s (2018) "time" dimension advances a teleology that combines the past, present, and future in one, and incorporates both the "problem" and "perspective" dimensions. The authors here borrow from systems engineering, with its explicit focus on history (legacy) as part of the environment that situates a problem and its potential solution(s). The scope of time within which problems are conceptualized is decisive, since definitions of a problem vary in relation to temporality. Depending on how far back critical reflection (hindsight) extends, reasoning—as embedded in the sum total of past experience across scale (individual to collective)—will yield differing points of departure and frames of reference. The intersections between problem, perspective, and time also extend forward and project into the future, with the consequences that predictive ability (foresight) has for long- versus short-term solutions. To reiterate and be clear, all three dimensions—problem, perspective, and time—of this systems thinking framework are intricately intertwined, and demand flexible and iterative (collaborative) metacognitive reasoning that deliberately examines interrelations between phenomena in question (Grohs et al., 2018).

A customary systems thinking mental map used for understanding complex global problems includes the iceberg model (see figure 4.2 below). It illustrates the importance that framing and gaps in perception play when

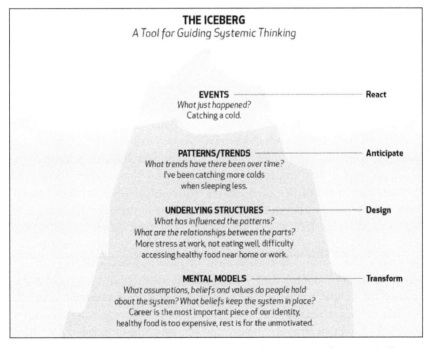

THE ICEBERG
A Tool for Guiding Systemic Thinking

EVENTS ——————————— **React**
What just happened?
Catching a cold.

PATTERNS/TRENDS ——————————— **Anticipate**
What trends have there been over time?
I've been catching more colds
when sleeping less.

UNDERLYING STRUCTURES ——————————— **Design**
What has influenced the patterns?
What are the relationships between the parts?
More stress at work, not eating well, difficulty
accessing healthy food near home or work.

MENTAL MODELS ——————————— **Transform**
What assumptions, beliefs and values do people hold
about the system? What beliefs keep the system in place?
Career is the most important piece of our identity,
healthy food is too expensive, rest is for the unmotivated.

Figure 4.2. The Iceberg Model. *Source*: Reprinted with permission from Ecochallenge. org.

discerning phenomena. With only 10 percent of its mass in plain view above water, and 90 percent submerged under water, the iceberg symbolizes the overwhelming matter hidden from view. The depiction reveals the tip of the iceberg's behavior as determined by ocean currents that occur beneath water, out of view but acting on 90 percent of its mass. Used as a visual tool and cartography, the iceberg provides a graphic image of the layered, covert component parts of systems (i.e., ecosystems, organizations, institutions etc.), and is broken into four levels of thinking: at the first *event* level, participants are asked to describe what happened (the event); at the second *pattern* level, participants identify trends that have existed over time; at the third *structure* level, participants distinguish factors that influence identified trends and patterns; and at the fourth *mental model* level, participants reflect on underlying assumptions, beliefs, and values that people hold about the system (Ecochallenge, n.d.).

Projecting forward to envision action-oriented change, the four levels of thinking correspond with human agency and ability to (1) react: describe and define the event or what happened, (2) anticipate: project possibilities using identified patterns, (3) design: devise solutions based on identified relationships between patterns and parts, and (4) transform: identify mental models and address underlying (root) problems. Figure 4.3 on the opposite page features a rendition of the cultural iceberg analogy (my design), following Edward Hall's (1977) cultural iceberg model.

In the mid-1970s, Hall reasoned that external aspects of culture—which include conscious behaviors, traditions, and mores—represent but the tip of the iceberg. Beneath the surface, or internally and subconsciously, are aspects of culture that underlie behavior and traditions, including beliefs and values that are often unconscious. Debates over Hall's characterization of "high" versus "low" context (nonverbal) communication across cultures notwithstanding[1] (Kittler et al., 2011), his seminal work on the integral role of culture for communication and meaning illustrates the influence it has on how we (differently) perceive and understand matter (Adler, 2003).

The illustration in figure 4.3 is designed to guide open-ended brainstorming and a mapping exercise in which participants (students) collectively ideate and identify forces that impinge upon behavior and practices related to climate change. Once a behavior or practice is specified, students collaboratively articulate the explicit and more visible surface attributes of the behavior or practice, before moving on to the more hidden, deep attributes. Using gendered consumption as an example, how does con-

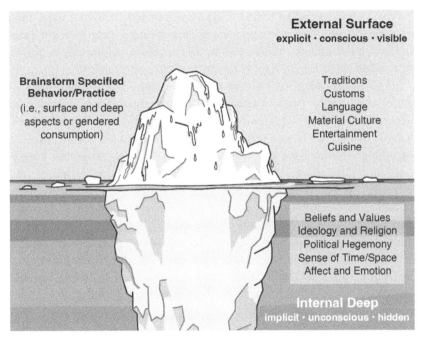

External Surface
explicit · conscious · visible

Brainstorm Specified Behavior/Practice

(i.e., surface and deep aspects or gendered consumption)

Traditions
Customs
Language
Material Culture
Entertainment
Cuisine

Beliefs and Values
Ideology and Religion
Political Hegemony
Sense of Time/Space
Affect and Emotion

Internal Deep
implicit · unconscious · hidden

Figure 4.3. Using the Iceberg Model of Culture. *Source*: Created by the author.

sumption differentially manifest in varied locations in relation to gender ideology and identity? What are some differences in consumption patterns between females, males, or those who identify as gender nonconforming? How do these patterns relate to surface traditions and, in turn, deeper, more hidden, and often unconscious aspects of cultural life? In what ways are local histories, socioeconomics, and politics enmeshed in identified behavior patterns?

The results will no doubt vary, depending on student cultural backgrounds, perspectives and understandings, but will allow students to enter into dialogue about, and begin teasing out, the meanings and worldviews that influence vectors of climate change at a deeper level. It is important to note that although the surface-versus-deep attributes in figure 4.3 above are dichotomously organized, they need not be confined to either of the surface-deep divide. This confirms the significance of mental mapping as a means to transcend rather than reinforce the grip of "ideal types"

(Weber, 1949)—as when heuristic typology becomes reified as more than constructed taxonomies. In other words, surface and/or deep level attributes of the cultural iceberg model need not be conceived as mutually exclusive, but rather allow for overlap, entanglement, and adaptability.

Complex, adaptive systems approaches reinforce the relevancy of social cartography (mental maps) for experimenting with intercultural, generative ways of seeing, thinking, and knowing when tackling convoluted subject matter. A systems thinking approach illuminates the significance of problem-framing for problem-solving, while recognizing that knowledge and solutions are diverse, incomplete (hidden, transforming), and imperfect (Grohs et al., 2018; Kolko, 2015; Liedtka, 2015). It furthermore underscores the importance of integrating imaginaries from across hard and soft science divides—as explored earlier—including "engineering education, critical thinking literature in philosophy, . . . and scholarship related to leadership and community development, organizational studies, and public policy" (Grohs et al., 2018, p. 111). To this list we can add important fields of study from the humanities and social sciences (i.e., history, literature, anthropology, sociology, psychology, and so forth), but also, more specifically, action-oriented theories of change (TOC) that summon the collaborative competency explored in chapter 3, and that allow us to think beyond sedimented structures and theoretical reasoning.

It bears mentioning that despite their significance as guideposts for community organizing and social mobilization, theories of change (TOC) come in many varieties. Stein (2019b) pushes back against predominant theories of change that characterize contemporary problems as "contingent failures of an otherwise solid set of institutions and ideas" (p. 668). Theories of change based in decolonizing perspectives and aspirations, by contrast, understand the challenges facing us as the result of unsustainable systems that are violent and destructive at root (Stein 2019b; Byrd, 2011; Rodriguez, 2018; Silva, 2014; Tuck & Yang, 2012). In efforts to expand our field of vision, Stein (2019b) provides a mental map juxtaposing three decolonial theories of change in relation to their intended reach: minor reform, major reform, and beyond reform. If we are to avoid remaining prisoners of provincial thinking, disjointed systems, and blinkered structures, our view must venture into the realm of "messy, collective process[es] of learning/unlearning that . . . lead . . . to viable, but as-yet-undefined and unimaginable [non-liner] futures" (Stein, 2019b, p. 673). In other words, theories of change that encourage experimentation beyond the contours of established discourse and imaginaries allow us to explore and engage different possibilities.

Table 4.1. Theories of Change Table

	Minor reform	**Major reform**	**Beyond reform**
Emphasis of change	Doing differently	Knowing differently	Being differently
Theory of change	Improve the effectiveness, efficiency, and inclusiveness of the existing system	Pluralize knowledge and representation, and enact redistribution of resources within existing system	Learn from/at the limits of the existing system, experiment with and regenerate other possibilities
Horizon of hope	Perpetual expansion and improvement toward greater progress, and exporting the system to other countries	Learning from alternative ways of knowing in search of roadmaps that can lead toward more equitable, sustainable futures	Messy, collective process of learning/ unlearning that might lead (non-linearly) to viable but as-yet-undefined and unimaginable futures
Response to the crumbling house	Maintain and operate the house more efficiently (e.g. install solar panels, improve insulation), invite in a few more people	Remodel and expand the house to invite many more, different people inside, democratize house governance, and use sustainable materials	Dismantle the house and/ or witness its inevitable collapse, learn from its mistakes, and experiment with building other kinds of dwellings
Response to crises of higher education	Reclaim public good purposes, flatten the "playing field" for social mobility, toward a diversified (global) middle class	Radically transform existing institutions by redistributing material resources, opportunities, and epistemic authority to the most marginalized	Mitigate harm and redistribute in the short- term, and consider what might be possible beyond "the university as we know it" in the long-term

Source: Stein, 2019b, p. 673. Reprinted by permission of the publisher (Taylor & Francis).

The existential questions that accompany complexity, ambiguity, and uncertainty corroborate long-standing awareness that "social problems are never solved . . . [but rather] re-solved—over and over again" (Rittel & Webber, 1973, p. 160). They also corroborate more recent calls to resist retrofitting complexity, contradiction, and conflict to suit "coherent, normative formulas with . . . unambiguous agendas" in a frenzy for solutions (Andreotti et al., 2015, p. 22). The difficulty, of course, involves our discomfort with uncertainty, the unknown, and what is "yet-to-be-defined," and surrendering the comforts of complicity (Shotwell, 2016). Equally difficult is our (un)willingness to relinquish control and concede to the ambiguity of things "fundamentally outside our control" (Shotwell, 2016, p. 8). These and related challenges resound a constellation of concerns that have crystallized as part of post-normal Science (PNS) and its scholarship since the mid-1980s.

Often traced to the work of Silvio Funtowicz and Jerome Ravetz, and their landmark publication *Science for the Post-Normal Age* (1993), PNS has been described as a collection of different approaches to policy-related science that "are critical and reflective, uncertainty-aware, quality-focused, foster plurality in scientific and normative perspectives on complex issues, and actively engage extended peer communities in the production, appraisal and use of knowledge" (Dankel et al., 2017, p. 1). Many of the goals, norms, and values that surface in post-normal discourse resonate with vocabulary found across complexity and systems theory. As a point of reference, the review article by Kønig et al. (2017) identifies a total of 33 prototypical norms and values featured in 397 PNS publications, organized around the core value of sustainability: quality, robustness, inclusiveness, democratization of expertise, adaptability, flexibility, creativity, holism, pluralism, integration, awareness, reflexivity, humility, relevance, applicability, precaution, transparency, traceability, openness, accountability, intelligibility, accessibility, honesty, trust, responsibility, safety, dignity, mutual understanding, tolerance, equity, empowerment, and integrity (p. 17).[2]

Post-normal science aims to democratize scientific expertise and expand its peer community in order to accommodate "a plurality of legitimate perspectives, value dissent, high stakes, and decision urgency" (Kønig et al., 2017, p. 13). Extending the peer community entails collaborating across scientific fields and encouraging multidisciplinary work, but also including all stakeholders in decisions about how problems are framed, conceptualized, and evaluated (Kønig et al., 2017). As Kønig et al.

(2017) explain, "The extended peer community involves broader notions of facts, including for example leaked documents, local experiences, and information provided by investigative journalists (Funtowicz & Ravetz, 1992, 1993). These 'extended facts' are highly relevant for the problem framing process and the choices of indicators" (p. 13).

The PNS emphasis on democratizing scientific expertise overlaps with participatory paradigms that have emerged in various fields of expertise, including design thinking (DT)—with its significant influence on neighboring disciplines. Intentionally integrating end users (participants, community members) into design, DT is known for relying on inclusive generative processes for framing, thinking about, and solving problems. The approach ultimately spread beyond the field of physical object design, to action, systems design, and even social organizational management (Groh et al., 2018; Brown & Martin, 2015). The participatory and democratic design of such emergent modalities resemble extant research praxis that centerstage collaborative creativity, and that situate those most affected by problems at the center of problem-solving (i.e., participatory community-based research, participatory action research).

It deserves mentioning that post-normal science is not intended as contravention to "normal" science. As Kønig et al. (2017) note, it seeks to complement rather than substitute for "normal" science. This confirms an all-hands-on-deck approach when confronting pressing problems that are increasingly designated "wicked." Because wicked problems involve thorny, compound issues that beckon integrated analyses of multifarious factors, problem-solving cannot remain isolated to scientific expertise and technical innovation. Systems thinking, complexity theory, and related paradigms provide a starting point for understanding problems as comprised by a plurality of intricate parts that continually adjust, and for identifying causal patterns through time and space. Although the field is crowded by various schools of thought,[3] theorizing congeals around a shared vision and belief in fundamental systems principles: that the relationship between problem and causality is often far from obvious (direct); that we often unwittingly contribute to problems and can influence outcomes by changing behavior; that quick fixes can have unintended, aggravating consequences; that improving the "whole" requires improving relationships between its "parts"; and that coordinated changes sustained over time can produce significant systems change (Stroh, 2015, p. 15).

This shared vision reflects the systems competencies that UNESCO identifies for bringing proactive sustainability responses into the fold across disciplinary divides: "the ability to recognize and understand relationships, to analyze complex systems, to perceive the ways in which systems are embedded within different domains and different scales, and to deal with uncertainty" (Leicht et al., 2018, p. 44). The following section narrows in the last of these: how we manage, or do not manage, uncertainty and lack of control in a VUCA world where preoccupation with "prediction, control and complete understanding are always an illusion" (Allen & Boulton, 2011, p. 178). Said differently, complexity theory and systems thinking are indispensable, but cannot deliver absolute truths, definitive roadmaps, control over the unknown, or command of the future.

Learning to Not Know in a VUCA World

A bird doesn't sing because it has an answer, its sings because it has a song.

—Maya Angelou

Southern New Hampshire University President Paul LeBlanc (2018) paints a bleak picture of the nation's current university system, with its top-heavy, hierarchical tilt ("shared governance" notwithstanding), rigid departmental boundaries-cum-territorial tensions, and sluggish pace of institutional change. This stands in stark and outdated contrast to the agility and nimble organizational shapeshifting needed to keep pace with the contemporary world. Against the backdrop of looming climate change, world social and political turmoil, and gross disparities in wealth, the Fourth Industrial Revolution stands at our doorstep. Machine intelligence and technology "are transforming almost every field of human endeavor" writes LeBlanc, and although "we do have a little time to rethink what we do," we do not have "a lot of time given the velocity of change" (2018, p. 23).

This presents formidable challenges for higher education, with its deeply entrenched traditions and ritual requirements. The fluidity and amorphous landscape brought about by technological advance and accelerating change will require future students to move more swiftly in and out of a learning environment, according to LeBlanc, and complete pieces of an educational whole in more flexible segmented parcels. Among the formal learning possibilities he envisions are micro-credentials, immersive simulations, repurposing, and retooling, which will take place in ongoing spurts over a lifetime and be officiated by globally distributed blockchain technology. Conventional degrees, he predicts, will remain but part of the equation in a far more malleable learning ecosystem (LeBlanc, 2018).

LeBlanc's prophecies presage both hope and alarm. We can hope that the adaptations described give way to more forgiving pathways for non- and post-traditional learners—many comprising marginalized groups of people struggling with the compound burdens that widening inequities have brought about and that COVID-19 only exacerbated. The system of higher education as we know it is ill-equipped to assist this group of students—financially, substantively, remedially, emotionally—yet they are poised to make up a significant percentage of the shifting student demographic on its way. They are the students often squeezed out of elite programs, arriving by way of less esteemed and circuitous learning pathways (community colleges, multiple institutions) and struggling to compensate for underresourced and underperforming educational backgrounds, as they patch together "second-rate" degree completion programs.

Higher education remains a highly segregated system, revealing the myth of meritocracy and social mobility, and dismal investment in one of the foremost public institutions upon which democracy and the growing masses of those with few means depend. We can hope the momentum of competency-based education, experiential learning, service learning, and similar praxis-oriented modalities will better capture the wealth of knowledge that diverse, "nontraditional" students contribute to their learning environments. Community-based education in particular has gained traction as a "common language and tool for aligning" learning and transferable skills with diversified workforce needs (LeBlanc, 2018, p. 24). Many nontraditional students arrive to the classroom endowed with untapped wisdom and expertise, by way of their varied cultural, life, and professional experiences, much of which gets lost to the rules, rituals, and filters of institutionalized learning. As an example, one of my students in a course featuring content on restorative justice (RJ) had worked several years in an after-school program where RJ was the practice for navigating conflict among participating youth. Her hands-on experience with RJ in a workplace setting contributed invaluable insights and expertise as part of our classroom deliberations.

LeBlanc anchors his analysis in the realities of a VUCA world, a world where volatility, uncertainty, complexity, and ambiguity rule. At the risk of lending further support to militarized perspectives that predominate in far too many contemporary narratives, the VUCA vocabularies warrant both serious consideration and critical scrutiny. Coined by the U.S. military and first introduced "after the end of the cold war to describe the conditions of a world ever more difficult to predict and rely on" the acronym was ultimately adapted by business and management across industries after the 2008–2009 Great Recession (Schick et al., 2017, p. 1). As Schick et al. (2017) contend, organizations across the globe suddenly faced conditions comparable to a battlefield or war room, with their social and economic circumstances shaped by daunting VUCA attributes. More and more, organizations and institutions are urged to plan with "uncertainty, indeterministic tendencies, emergent properties, . . . non-linear relationships and feedback processes" in mind (Schick et al., 2017, p. 2). The push to plan for an uncertain and complex future remains indiscriminately prefaced on knowledge authority and predictability, however, and fails to appreciate that "knowability" is inherently limited by the exponential complexity of intertwined socioeconomic and natural systems (Schick et al., 2017, p. 2).

Schick et al. (2017) sketch a descriptive delineation of each VUCA attribute, with the first of these—*volatility*—defined as the "rate of change (usually rapid), and the pattern of dynamics observed in socioenvironmental systems" (p. 7). As clear and concise as this definition reads, the attribute is characterized by increasing "speed of interactions and . . . growth of linkages between elements in biophysical, technical, and human systems at a number of spatial scales" (Schick et al., 2017, p. 7). As a result, it remains ever more difficult to determine and manage with any exactitude the elements and interactive dynamics within systems of change (Schick et al., 2017; Held, 2000; Young et al., 2006). Despite the abundant evidence of nonlinearity and unpredictability in both natural and cultural systems (market fluctuations, technological innovation, climate change), however, many of the conceptual models we rely on across industries continue to be moored in closed system models and "static state" principles (Schick et al., 2017, p. 7).

Along similar lines, Schick et al. (2017) define *uncertainty* as "characterized by the lack of predictability and the likely prospects for surprise" (p. 7). Miller et al. (2018) further characterize this attribute in terms of circumstances for which the structure and variables of a problem may be a given, but knowledge of their value(s) remain undetermined. For all the unknowns that distinguish complex systems, their multifarious properties, points of interaction, and feedback loops at the very least promise the certainty of uncertainty (Schick et al., 2017; Holling, 1978; Walters, 1986; Gunderson et al., 1995; Gunderson & Holling, 2002). The irony, again, is that so much science and expertise continues to portray conceptual models as if "the necessary knowledge of most, if not all, of the elements" are at our disposal (Schick et al., 2017, p. 7).

Despite the overall low-level success of ecological and sociopolitical predictive models, a high level of trust remains vested in expert knowledge and authority. One adverse upshot of this bestowed trust is that participant agents are faced with (and unprepared for) much higher levels of uncertainty than expected. Although people by and large gravitate toward the reassurance that knowledge authority lends, exposure to dynamic adaptive and open-ended approaches accustom us to the realities of uncertainty. Schick et al. (2017) thus underscore the high cost of problem-solving practices that rely on deterministic knowledge-based evidence "at the expense of non-knowledge-based" evidence (p. 8). In short, the intransigent relevancy and possibilities of all that we *do not* know deserves far more deliberate attention.

Explored in part in the previous section, the *complexity* VUCA attribute is defined by Schick et al. (2017) as "the intricate and extensive network structure and dynamic pathways existing between the components of a system" (p. 8). It goes without saying that complexity involves innumerable confounding factors when determining cause and effect, particularly the further apart interlinkages between components are in space and time (Schick et al., 2017; Levin, 1999). Complexity increases as component parts and interconnections of systems increase and as feedback loops between properties and potential causal links multiply. Long periods of delay between cause and effect, and the diverse perspectives and interpretations of intervening participants (human agents), further convolute these intricacies. The more inclusive our perspective, over space and time, the more imperfect and impertinent measurability and predictability become. All this makes plain the challenges of pinpointing predictive solutions with any certainty. The temporal and collaborative dimensions of the 3C cartography confirm the need to think along a "wide range of spatial and temporal scales over which ecological systems are structured and operate," and amid which humans configure but a miniscule, although increasingly detrimental, part in the Anthropocene (Schick et al., 2017, p. 8).

Of all the VUCA attributes, Schick et al. (2017) characterize *ambiguity* as the most abstract: "the haziness of reality, the potential for misreads, the mixed meanings of conditions, and the mixed outcomes of actions" (p. 9). The concept has been further described as situations involving "novelty, complexity, insolubility, unpredictability and uncertainty with a set of cognitive, emotional and behavioral reactions" (Grenier et al., 2005, as quoted in Tauritz, 2012, p. 300). The differing perspectives, with their varied interpretations, alongside the ubiquitous presence of ambiguity as part of nature, render precise definitions of *ambiguity* no more than tenuous (Schick et al., 2017). At best, scholars are able to depict real-world examples of the unexpected outcomes that ambiguity occasion *after the fact*. Reyer et al. (2012), for instance, cite as an example the unanticipated underbelly of renewable energy policies adopted in the EU, where government incentive to cultivate energy crops gave way to corn monoculture production, disrupting local biodiversity.

The intertwined patchwork of multidimensional interacting elements, adaptive systems, and feedback loops that characterize VUCA attributes reveal endless uncertainties that disrupt reductionist conjecture. Among the uncertainties that Allen and Boulton (2011) identify in "Complexity and Limits to Knowledge" are

> the behaviour between individual elements inside [a] system; . . . the collective behavior of [a] system; . . . how [a] system interacts with other systems; . . . the boundaries of what we define as a system or systems; . . . the environment in which [a] system is immersed and the way the system responds to change within this environment; and, . . . how the description of elements, system or the environment may change over time." (p. 165)

Building on the early work of Knight (1921), the authors insist that the "unknown unknown" is "associated with underlying structures and constructs [that are] themselves shifting, or disappearing . . . [with] new ones appearing" (Allen & Boulton, 2011, p. 173), and therefore cannot be ascertained.

Despite all the evidence to the contrary, however, dominant perspectives continue to present the world as objectively measurable, predictable, and controllable (Allen & Boulton, 2011, p. 165). This engrained point of departure wields persistent influence across various schools of thought and industry sectors, including policy and planning, the economy, management, development, education, and more (Allen & Boulton, 2011, p. 165). Scholars have been critical of economics in particular, as a field that encourages a false sense of certainty and predictable relationships between markets and the external conditions (social, environmental) in which they are embedded (Allen & Boulton, 2011). Allen and Boulton (2011) pinpoint the significance of complexity theory in bringing about more comprehensive economic models, including evolutionary economics (Nelson & Winter, 1982; Metcalfe, 2007), ecological economics (Boulding, 1950/1981; Georgescu-Roegen, 1971; Daly, 1999; Costanza et al., 2007), behavioral economics (Simon, 1955), and complexity economics (Beinhocker, 2007). Overall, their critique of classical science advocates for an ontology of uncertainty, and decoupling understanding from predictability—that we refrain from conflating understanding with efforts to predict the future (Allen & Boulton, 2011). Predictive approaches that elude the realities of uncertainty and "limits to knowledge" are problematic, because they prioritize understandings that suggest a false sense of control (Allen & Boulton, 2011, p. 164).

Although measuring and predicting uncertainty (aka risk assessment) remain central to science and knowledge accumulation, we cannot measure or quantify "true uncertainty" (Tauritz, 2012; Knight, 1921). Epistemological questions about how we address uncertainty—how we explore, ignore, or deny uncertainty—destabilize reductive assumptions that evade learning and knowledge exploration outside the realm of measurability (Allen & Boulton, 2011, p. 164). A strong argument can thus be made for the need to improve our tolerance of uncertainty, including knowledge uncertainty. Uncertainty is ubiquitous in nature and life, and determination to defeat its existence foreclose what we might otherwise be able to envision. But an argument in favor of uncertainty tolerance can also be made because of the emotional distress it can have when unexpected unknowns catch us off guard. In other words, it behooves us to improve our tolerance of the unknown even when we least expect it. The pertinence of uncertainty for emotional state of mind has become more than a passing preoccupation for growing numbers of people, as reflected in rising rates of mental health problems worldwide (World Health Organization, 2017).[4]

Levels of depression and anxiety have skyrocketed around the world in recent years, particularly among youth and college students and in response to the COVID-19 pandemic, with adverse implications for the cognitive, emotional, and social competencies needed to navigate academic experiences and expectations (J. Hoffman, 2020; Kwai & Peltier, 2021; Zraick, 2019). The increasing uncertainty and ambiguity that accompany accelerating change, technological advance, workforce obsolescence, and employment insecurity, more generally, have done little to soothe the unease, and are often cast as contributing factors. Students need guidance and support to wade through the unchartered waters and rising tide of uncertainty characterizing contemporary life, including the social class known as the *precariat* (Standing, 2016). For college students and recent graduates, dwindling prospects for steady employment and work precarity adds urgency to the need for uncertainty competences amid contested knowledge in "post-normal" (Funtowicz & Ravetz, 1993) times, all while we reassess how to negotiate scientific knowledge, value systems, and ubiquitous complexity (Tauritz, 2012).

Students enter into learning environments with varying thresholds for the unknown—not unlike their varying thresholds for cognitive dissonance (Festinger, 1957)—but must nonetheless find their place amid, and learn to live with, the realities of uncertainty. This involves metacognitive learning that recognizes and honors how individuals subjectively experience and differentially cope with shifting degrees and types of uncertainty: "what is stimulating to one person is frightening to another" (Tauritz, 2012, p. 302). Uncertainty overload can have paralyzing effects for anyone engaged in problem-solving, as can unfamiliarity with navigating uncertainty. For this reason Tauritz (2012) advocates preparing students for knowledge uncertainty earlier than has been typical as part of formal education. This runs counter to customary education design, however, which tends toward eliminating or containing uncertainty and ambiguity in order to shelter students from information they are "too young" to digest, and to ensure clarity and efficiency in learning (Tauritz, 2012; Visser & Visser, 2004).

Tauritz (2012) builds on research from across disciplinary fields (developmental psychology, cognitive and decision sciences, neurocognitive sciences, education for sustainable development, education sciences, and instructional design), and proposes a preliminary framework for guiding youth through knowledge uncertainty. Anchored in a series of principles and "uncertainty competences" (several of which already are well established within education and ESD) the framework emphasizes embracing uncertainty; reflection skills and a flexible mindset; finding and evaluating information; assessing knowledge authorities; reasoning abilities; understanding probabilities; assessing your own abilities; engaging in supportive networks; and ability to anticipate and prepare for uncertainty. In short, the omnipresence of uncertainty in life and learning has prompted scholars to infuse uncertainty management as part of knowledge acquisition, workforce training, and professional development, with the concept of "positive uncertainty" (Gelatt, 1989)—borrowed from counseling—(re)gaining foothold.

For those familiar with assessment and student learning outcomes (SLOs), reading through the provisional list of uncertainty-related competences above makes clear that integrating "uncertainty education" need not involve overhauling existing curricula. Many of the learning goals included are common components in core curricula that span grade levels of formal education in Western societies. Tauritz (2012) contends that uncertainty competences require honing, however, and better assimilation as part of formal learning. The first two competences (embracing uncertainty and flexible, reflexive mindset) are particularly significant for this discussion. The predictive and teleological models commonly used as heuristic devices for understanding complex and/or unknown phenomena are indispensable to knowledge acquisition, but should not be conceived of as "methods of reducing uncertainty" (Tauritz, 2012, p. 304). The sense of control that reducing uncertainty lends notwithstanding, a false sense of certainty circumvents the importance of learning "*to tolerate uncertainty* and to remain open to new information" (Tauritz, 2012, p. 304).

Tauritz (2012) explains that uncertainty competency builds on both knowledge skills and attitude, and that adaptability and resisting the need for certainty are crucial when learning to tolerate uncertainty (p. 306). Generating new knowledge builds on both prior knowledge and unknowns, and is facilitated by habituation processes that encourage tolerance for the uncertainties that accompany the unknown. We become more accustomed to and adept at managing the cognitive and emotional impact of uncertainty with exposure and practice. Openness of mind is instrumental for envisioning possibilities and identifying solutions amid the ambiguities that problem-solving generates. Just as important as an open and flexible mindset, however, is reflexivity: "being able to reflect on one's own or other's beliefs and being able to change personal beliefs" (Tauritz, 2012, p. 306). This resonates with central elements of the 3C explored in chapter 2—"Contemplative Criticality and Unlearning"—and the need for heightened reflexivity about epistemologies and ontologies of "knowing, being and relating" that are deeply embedded in histories of coloniality (Stein, 2019b, p. 670).

As a central task of colonial projects, taxonomies of all sorts along various scales have had profound and lasting effects on how we view the world, mediate information, structure society, and control our environment. As Shotwell (2016) explains, "classification and its effects are intimately biopolitical, addressing how to sort people, group them, and how to manage what effect these activities have on population and time" (p. 26). An ontology of uncertainty must labor to uproot genealogies and upend historically constructed classifications, the false categories that we do not recognize as such, because they have fundamentally shaped our social relations and organization for so long that we no longer explicitly perceive them, but instead assume as commonsense their logic (Shotwell, 2016). This is the work that scholars and educators invested in decolonized learning engage in the classroom, that students may resist for fear of discomfort and facing feelings of shame, guilt, and responsibility, or that students may grieve when revisiting painful pasts that persist into the present.

This is also the work that breathes life into learning for students unable to identify themselves in mainstream education content, which remains far removed from their experiences. It is an ontology that labors to "listen to the sound of things not said" (Heffernan, 2015), whether hidden, suppressed, repressed, forbidden, omitted, evaded, disguised, or invisiblized. The following student reflection in response to Peggy McIntosh's (2010) classic "White Privilege: Unpacking the Invisible Knapsack" illustrates the layered complexity and murky residual effects that historic classifications have for self-identification and social relations in the contemporary classroom:

> I see Peggy's [McIntosh] point on some of the conditions she listed as white privileges and perhaps reading this has opened my eyes to things I may have never even thought of. With that being said, as a white, middle-aged, single mother who works full-time and trying to finish my college degree, I think people are mistaken or even delusional about what it means to be white. The color of my skin is "white" and for that reason I feel that I am expected to work hard for my money, not receive public assistance, pay for my health insurance, and pay for my education and my children's education. Nothing is handed to me on a platter. I make too much to receive help from the government but yet I make too little to make ends meet. I believe there is a huge misconception of what advantages a middle-class white person has. In reflecting on some of the items listed in the article, the first one that stood out to me was "I can be pretty sure that my neighbors in such a location will be neutral or pleasant to me." Again, this is a complete misconception. . . . Some neighbors are not accepting and will go as far as not allowing our children to play together because we come from the "poor" end of town.

Not only do these reflections disclose gaps in historical knowledge about the central role of race in structuring social relations and access to opportunities, they simultaneously reveal perceived gaps in appreciation for the circumstances that predominate in the lives of many middle- and working-class people, regardless of race. The personal testimony sheds light on the intersecting gender and economic class realities that have long configured our lives in composite ways, alongside the competing priorities that social stratification creates and that often inhibit our ability to fathom common cause across fractured class structure.

How might we make more tangible the parallels between this student's fate as a single female head of household—who must hold down the fort alone on the lesser income that a gendered pay gap routinely imposes—and that of other exploited peoples located across variegated sectors of social stratification? Are our curricula and learning effectively able to distinguish the unpaid household labor single mothers perform—indeed most mothers perform worldwide, single or not—in assuming the responsibilities of reproducing society and raising members of the next generation? Despite the difficulties of identifying similarities between variants of oppression and the dangers of uniformly equating one version to another, the advantages that inequalities collectively confer to those in more advantaged positions comprise an interlocking matrix we are taught not to see (McIntosh, 2010). This matrix of domination (Collins, 1990) requires unveiling and unravelling as part of learning. The classifications that buttress racism, sexism, and heterosexism are not the same, yet as intersecting systems, their substantive impact overlaps in significant ways that are important to make intelligible.

In "Gesturing Towards Decolonial Futures," Stein et al. (2020) disaggregate the epistemological and ontological categories upon which modernity and its possibilities and impossibilities build in search of certainty, around which possibilities for "knowing, being and relating" are enabled or disabled (p. 62). The organizing principles around which categories of control (race, gender, sexuality, ability, etc.) are structured presume that "all beings exist as discrete entities," that they exist in uneven relations, and that these uneven relations reflect differences in value that are intrinsic in nature (Stein, 2019b, p. 671; Mika, 2019; Silva, 2014). Not only does this ontological rationality separate humans from each other, using hierarchies of domination and ownership that differentially value and devalue groups of people, they separate humans from nonhuman life, as well as mind from body and intellect from affect (Stein, 2019b, p. 671).

When the contradictions of establishment rationalities, and false certainties that structure modern-colonial ways of thinking, being, and relating (aka control) are challenged, the critiques are squandered (as threats to our existence) and suppressed from view (Stein et al., 2020). They are relegated to the silent yet lurid sound of things not said. The separability that structures modernity's conceptual architecture is not fact but political fiction, however. Humans, animals, and other living species remain interconnected and embedded "within a wider ecological metabolism whether they recognize it or not" (Stein, 2019b, p. 671; Alexander, 2005). This is the same ecological metabolism in which intellect and emotion are ultimately intertwined, contrary to customary conviction. The patriarchal model that disaggregates public from private spheres provides a prime example of fictitious separability, distinguishing between professional (male, objective, detached) and private (female, subjective, emotional) behavioral patterns-cum-expectations.

Why on earth should we be expected to be less than fully human (leave our emotions at home) when we step into the "professional" realm? Who establishes such expectations, by what logic, and toward what end? Although we may heed warning signs that counter the "Cartesian dream" (Pereira & Funtowicz, 2015) in theory, the road is long to reinscribe habits of thinking and being that do not divorce body from mind or intellect from affect. Despite the mind's ability to forewarn against perceived threat and harm, for instance, our emotional sensibilities, desires, and visceral responses often gesture otherwise. Similarly, despite perfectly perceiving a problem, mobilizing for change—toward building something new and different—can be difficult because we continue chasing the (false) promises of "pleasure, comfort and security" associated with existing ways of being and doing (Stein, 2019b, p. 679). Said otherwise, although we might recognize that shallow promises of pleasure, comfort, and security fail to deliver, emotion can override intellect and the cognition upon which decision-making (and science) relies.

To summarize, negotiating climate change and its enormous challenges brings any number and unpredictable combinations of complexity, ambiguity, and volatility to the forefront, discrediting the validity of scientific precision or certainty. Navigating VUCA imaginaries requires flexible cognition that not only accommodates cultural and historical differentiation across disparate landscapes, but also vastly varied sensibilities, affects, and intuitions (Tauritz, 2012; Gelatt 1989; Kaufman, 1999). Excavating the contingencies and plasticity of diverse knowledge foundations destabilizes familiar frames of reference, and demands intentional deliberation that integrates uncertainty competence as a critical component of learning. If they are to distinguish fact from fiction, navigate the ethical limits of cultural relativism, and find common ground amid ubiquitous indeterminacy, students and faculty need opportunities to explore the values, worldviews, and preconceptions that inform their thinking. Complexity theory, adaptive systems theory, and cultivating uncertainty tolerance are significant starting points, but require classroom experimentation and risk-taking (Tauritz, 2012; DeRoma et al., 2003). Such experimentation entails that we nurture learning ecosystems that are more forgiving of imperfection, failure, and vulnerability.

Complexity, uncertainty, and ambiguity mean different things for different people in different situations which, in turn, hinge on differences in how knowledge authorities and meanings are framed (Tauritz, 2012; Van Asselt, 2000). The purpose of this chapter and its 3C competency (comprehensive complexity) is not to advance the science of complexity as a means to conquer uncertainty in the VUCA battlefield of complicated unknowns, nor necessarily to undermine the significance of probability, systematic observation, or measurement. It is to move toward an ontology of uncertainty that draws attention to and recognizes the inseparable dimensions along which knowledge and understanding is generated and consolidates—cognitive, emotional, relational, cultural, existential, spiritual, ecological, and so forth. It is to reconnect disaggregated connections between the many dimensions that necessarily nourish comprehension, knowledge acquisition, and understanding. It is to acknowledge that we need more generous and merciful models to help us live in harmony with, draw inspiration from, and heed the force of things unknown.

But it is also to acknowledge that although "prediction, control and complete understanding are always an illusion" (Allen & Boulton, 2011, p. 178), uncertainty and unpredictability do not preclude using perception and predictability to experiment with modeling. The alternative—to not experiment with models—is not desirable, nor an option, since thinking is "itself . . . a form of modeling" (Allen & Boulton, 2011, p. 178). The 3C cartography experimented with in this book is an invitation to "adopt a pragmatic approach to models and see them as [living] experiments in representation, where we retain those that seem useful and continue to modify those that fail, treating all as an adjunct to thinking and not as defining 'the answer'" (Allen & Boulton, 2011, pp. 178–179). Experimentation is by definition risky. It risks that our attempts go wrong or in ways we do not anticipate. In short, experimentation must prepare for predictions and models that fail. To return to LeBlanc's (2018) forecast at the beginning of this chapter, we need "innovation spaces in which stakeholders can try new things and fail . . . without penalty and recrimination" (p. 25). This commands generosity and grace when our experimentation, expectations, and aspirations fail. Before moving to the final chapter, I expound on the need to nurture rather than foreclose failure—with compassion—and to destabilize the arrogance of excellence that separability (individualism) animates.

Arrogance of Excellence and the Right to Be Wrong

> I have not failed 10,000 times—I've successfully found 10,000 ways that will not work.
>
> —Thomas Edison

There is something profoundly problematic about the aspirations of "excellence" in which contemporary models of teaching, learning, and innovation are steeped. As the cornerstone of formal knowledge acquisition, tropes of excellence set a deceptive tenor for what learning means and does not mean, for how we learn about ourselves, from each other, and as part of the communities we belong to. What exactly is excellence, how do we measure it, and who establishes the criteria we use to assess it? If years upon years of education reform have taught us anything, it is that no manner of rebranding, in theory or taxonomy, will bring about excellence, whatever its definition. Were we to take the idle warnings and canting of diversity, equity, and inclusion (DEI) to heart (or their logical conclusion), excellence becomes a misnomer. If it is incumbent upon us to genuinely celebrate diversity of all kinds, then intellectual, creative, physical, or other manifestations of talent and aptitude each become one among many types of diverse abilities, prized along false hierarchies of value. This is not to argue against celebrating abilities of all and diverse kinds. It is to argue that we need to think critically about our aspirational benchmarks, values, and instruments of measurement.

The hidden hierarchies of value that tropes of excellence belabor have a way of discouraging criticality, the vulnerability that comes with doubt, and the humility that facilitates openness of mind. As a result, learning to be wrong, to be amenable to other options, to be exposed, and to *not* be excellent are inhibited. For some educators, excellence is a fetish involving narrowly conceived learning goals that prioritize cognitive skills over substantive proficiencies embedded in identity, culture, history, and affect. Literacy scholar Gholdy Muhammad (2020) warns against the recursive thrust of curricular design that perpetuates mainstream frameworks and content, and that advances rote skills in the abstract. Her argument insists on diversifying learning content and infusing criticality, dialectical learning, and agitation throughout education, so that students recognize themselves in the curriculum and their cultural, gender, sexual, and racial identities are affirmed rather than erased or devalued (Noguera, 2003; Muhammad, 2020).

To learn is ultimately to collaborate, to enter into academic dialogue, and to collaborate is to learn to know yourself—your cultural, historical, sociopolitical, racialized, gendered self—in relation to others like you but also in relation to the "histories and truths of other diverse people" (Muhammad, 2020, p. 67). That knowledge accumulation is collaborative at its core (generative and collectively created) is particularly relevant for groups of people who have been oppressed or discriminated against. Muhammad (2020) documents the historically cooperative nature of knowledge and literacy among people of color in the United States, and explains that literary societies "were highly collaborative and prompted social responsibility to share knowledge gained . . . rather than keep education to one's self" (p. 26). Such notions of knowledge as collective and collaborative contradict existing structures and conceptualizations of education as embedded in individualism and competition, however (Muhammad, 2020). In other words, the conditions in which "excellence" in ideation and innovation are ideally borne out are antithetical to the insular ambition that individualism and competition superimpose.

Muhammad rounds out learning and knowledge-building as crucial to shaping our individual and social identities, our understandings of ourselves, the communities to which we belong, and the world—none of which materialize through standardized lessons, formulaic assessment, catchy reform acronyms, or cosmetic rebranding (2020). She reviews the lessons that Black historical literary societies taught us (Muhammad, 2020, pp. 32–35):

- learning must be responsive to people's lives and the social events that shape their lives;

- people with diverse experiences and backgrounds learn from one another when they use each other's perspective as a resource;

- learning must be situated in an intentionally collaborative, shared space;

- learning must engage with the power and authority within which text and knowledge is necessarily immersed;

- knowledge acquisition is developed alongside identity and intellectual development;

- learning must be tied to "joy, love, and aesthetic fulfillment."

As part of the long arc of democratic education and lifelong learning—to bring about meaning and human flourishing—the liberatory and humanizing impact of reading, writing, thinking, and learning provide crucial "access to mental freedom, political power, and agenda building" (Muhammad, 2020, p. 19). In the age of mass incarceration (aka the New Jim Crow), notions of mental freedom, and the liberatory and (re) humanizing effects of learning, take on particular meanings for people in prison pursuing a "life examined" (Socrates) through studying with others. Philosopher Damon Horowitz (2011) describes learning from his philosophy student in San Quentin State Prison, whose body is in prison but mind is freed. In arguing that Kant's moral categorical imperative is too "uncompromising to deal with the conflict that affects our everyday," the student questions if we are "condemned to moral failure" (Horowitz, 2011). Horowitz does not have the answer, but invites his student in a shared exploration of the considerations this question provokes. He reminds his students and us to be wise enough to know how little we know (aka humility).

Benchmarks of excellence are in this context turned on their head. In prison, the cultural contingencies of success (excellence) and the failure(s) against which it is measured are inverted and become more visible. Excellence and success assume new life-forms. The mindlessness of formal skills development emerges as the antithesis of thoughtfulness. Excellence is nothing if not value-laden and moral in nature. Rather than seek out the wisdom of unknown or unfamiliar ways of seeing, thinking, and being in the world, tropes of excellence often evade questioning established imaginaries, however. Liberating the mind means deconstructing what we believe and why we believe it (Horowitz, 2011). By failing to push back against the power, status, and cultural tropes that carefully or carelessly curate truths we hold dear or presume as fact, they capitulate to exclusionary knowledge (re)production.

Students deserve to grow (in body, mind, and soul), to grow old enough to vote (absent felony disenfranchisement or police killings), and to nourish meaningful relationships with those different than themselves (Muhammad, 2020). In so doing, they cultivate the habits of mind and diverse ways of thinking and knowing that living together in a global world requires. As one of my students in a combined class[5] in prison explained,

> I wanted to take a combined class to engage with people who were not like me so that they would know me and I them and that we would know more . . . about each other. This is exactly what happened. I learned that people are able to understand and share my feelings; that fear can be transposed into love. I learned that people can believe in you even at your lowest point and that by letting outsiders in, and vice versa, you open up doors; doors to understanding; doors that shut out judgment and exile and allow us to see the humanity in each other despite the circumstances we may find ourselves in.

As a Black female of West Indian descent, the student had grown up in a segregated community with little opportunity to move outside the racial and cultural contours of her neighborhood. She described her experience of engaging the same impressions her entire life, and her sense of enlightenment when interacting with people from backgrounds unlike her own—despite the uncertainty and discomfort that venturing outside familiar terrain entails. Her insights foreground the significance of diverse experiences for expanding worldviews, beyond the grip of things customary and convenient. Exposure to different ways of thinking, feeling, and being enables us to understand social phenomena, questions, problems, and reality from different vantage points. It allows us to distinguish and formulate alternative reasoning in our efforts to make sense of the world.

Preserving partial or insular truths exists in anachronistic tension to a fair and well-functioning plural democracy, no matter where in the world we are. Students who cannot recognize themselves in education content become disenfranchised from civic participation and political engagement; they have no point of entry into academic dialogue in which their identity, culture, and history is honored, and in relation to which they, in turn, may appreciate the identities, cultures, and histories of others. Equally important, insular truths obscure undesirable or unwelcome parts of reality, experience, and perspective—notably those that materialize from failure. The epigraph at the opening of this section is symptomatic of the uneasy alignment between failure and excellence. Thomas Edison did not fail, he "successfully found ways that will not work." We are versed in slogans like this, coined by our enlightened forefathers, that praise the noble feats of failure, yet are antithetical to persistent tropes of excellence. The systems of merit, reward, and recognition at the base of academics are diametrically opposed to the inclusion, acceptance, and support needed to fail well, and learn from failure. We are discouraged from shining light on failure.

Jessica Bennett's (2017) *New York Times* article about failure on the syllabus ("On Campus, Failure Is on the Syllabus") provides some poignant pointers. Contemporary students are anguished by the pressures to be perfect. The article features testimonials about the weight of competition and having to project the image of perfection. The expectations (real or perceived) that students succeed in all areas of life (academics, social life, romantic pursuits, family relations, friendships) place great burdens on their well-being. Expectations of perfection wind their way into such daily rituals as sleeping enough, exercising regularly, looking your best, and keeping up with social media. The appearance of perfection matters. In efforts to help students cope with the challenges of college and life, including the impact of failure, faculty have designed curricular content that incorporates failure. Such curricula avoids treating failure as an aberration in learning, elevating it to a central feature instead.

Including failure on the syllabus proves particularly meaningful for students who do not perform in line with conventional metrics of assessment. It has spawned programs that reward those courageous enough to pursue creative initiatives without guarantee of success. This begs the question of whether success can ever be guaranteed, but also why such an inordinate amount of emphasis is placed on success when failure proves so magnanimous: Thomas Edison found ten thousand ways that did *not* work before succeeding. Classroom explorations in failure do not always track well with everyone. In one of my courses, a middle-aged White male student shared his response to related coursework as follows: "cry me a river. . . . And then we are asked to share failures, uncertainty and vulnerability. I have a wife and a therapist that fulfills that part of my life. Maybe I let my emotions get the best of me after class on Wednesday, but I can only take so much of the psycho-babble. Life is a bowl of spaghetti."

Extravagant reactions aside, courage in ingenuity and innovation will not materialize if vulnerability and failure are discouraged in our learning calculus. We need to round out Halberstam's (2011) notion of "low theory" as an antidote to hegemonic modes of knowing (male, hetero, cis, White, etc.), and to contest normative knowledge orthodoxies that undermine creative possibility. We need to inspire generative spaces where susceptibility to error, rejection, and failure is not only encouraged but the ability (right) to be vulnerable and wrong becomes a measure of aptitude. This will by necessity implicate uncovering vastly varied archeology of our plural pasts. In the next and final chapter I explore the challenges of co-creating knowledge diversity embedded in variegated experiences and inclusive histories of the past, in order to envision and move toward common sustainable futures. Chapter 5 concludes the book with the importance of cultivating institutional structures, pedagogical approaches, and sites of learning where the risk of imperfection and failure, the enlightenment of historical reconciliation and healing, and the merits of mistakes may predominate.

Chapter Five

Otherwise Imaginaries

Beloved Sustainable Community

Martin Luther King Jr. had a global vision for his legendary notion of the *beloved community*, a vision where worldwide standards of human dignity and decency would dissuade poverty, hunger, and homelessness, and where "racism and all forms of discrimination, bigotry and prejudice [would] be replaced by an all-inclusive spirit of sisterhood and brotherhood" (King Center, n.d.). Rooted at the core of Dr. King's concept of community are economic and social justice, which in the first and final analysis affects everything from social status, life opportunities, residency, and general well-being, to stress hormone levels, health determinants, and life expectancy (Ritterman, 2017). Put differently, economic and social justice is an intrinsic measure of the overall health of a society, with impact on a wide range of outcomes for better or for worse. As Ritterman (2017) describes, in "highly unequal countries, like the United States, health outcomes and social well-being suffer" (para. 8).

The COVID-19 pandemic brought into sharp relief the struggles and strife that diverse peoples—within and between countries—experience, bear witness to, and must negotiate, before reacting to or acting on any wish or will to imagine and manifest alternative sustainable lifeways. According to the Sustainable Development Goals 2020 Report, the pandemic is reversing decades of advances in the areas of poverty, healthcare, and education across the world, rendering the 2030 agenda ever more challenging to achieve (UN Department of Economic and Social Affairs, 2020). COVID-19 has affected everyone, but it has not done so equally:

"instead, it has exposed and exacerbated existing inequalities and injustices. In advanced economies, fatality rates have been highest among marginalized groups. In developing countries, the most vulnerable . . . risk being hit even harder" (UN Department of Economic and Social Affairs, 2020). In short, the pandemic exposed profound inequalities that persist worldwide and has exacerbated disparities, disproportionately affecting Black and Brown communities and vulnerable groups of people. The asymmetries in outcome—in large part configured along racial and gendered lines—is a far cry from the beloved community Martin Luther King Jr. envisioned.

From a needs-based, pragmatic point of view, concerns over climate change and sustainability are likely to fall low on the list of priorities under circumstances of scarcity, deprivation, and suffering. This much was made viscerally clear during a sociology seminar on social and cultural change I taught at Bedford Hills Correctional Facility (a maximum security prison for women located in New York) some years ago. The course was organized around climate change and the impact of humans on the environment and earth's ecosystems, and explored strategies for sustainable social change that avert socioecological destruction. In examining our human footprint across various vectors—energy use, food systems, waste, transportation, urbanization—as situated within the particulars of diverse social and cultural contexts, students discussed their vested interest in lifestyle choices and behavior patterns in response to climate change. What forces and factors mediate behavior at a local and personal level, I asked, and how might we move toward shifts in thinking and action that mitigate anthropogenic drivers related to such lifestyle and behavior?

The answers were as candid as they were heartfelt and harrowing: How could you possibly consider whether your behavior is sufficiently sustainable if you are so clinically depressed that even getting out of bed is a distant dream? How could you possibly fathom sustainable food systems if you are terrified you won't be able to feed your children, at all? Why would you possibly entertain questions of sustainability if all your time and energy is consumed by drug addiction and unbearable withdrawal symptoms? But a glimpse into an abyss of individual narrative particulars, the responses conjure up inventories of privation. In world locations near and far, they signal poverty, hunger, and food insecurity; structural violence, domestic abuse, and warfare; police brutality, criminal injustice, and persecution; unemployment and homelessness; health disparities and alarming rates of mental health problems (the list goes on). As significant factors that impact drivers of climate change, lifestyle behaviors are fundamentally mediated by basic human needs that go unfulfilled and that override any potential agency people might muster to alter their ways.

I was reminded of Jody Lewen's (2012) Big Ideas Fest lecture and powerful description of the "many paths to prison," usually characterized by "at least some degree" of academic disqualification: "absent or addictive parents; physical violence; homelessness; hunger, exploitation and abuse. Parents are high on meth or crack, siblings are hungry, there are no clean diapers in the house. No one reads anybody a bedtime story or checks . . . homework." What does it mean, she asked, "to be paranoid when you've lived most of your life in the charge of people who really did hold you in contempt or who were at best utterly indifferent to your subjective experience or your needs?" (Lewen, 2012). The charge to save the earth and planetary ecosystems must galvanize all the people in our beloved community—as the human agents with power to sway drivers of climate change in the Anthropocene—by directing attention to the vast discrepancies that persist between those who do and do not have their essential needs satisfied. Only then will we liberate the energy, time, and mindset—shackled by privation—to envision, create, act on, and educate about alternative possibilities for our common sustainable future.

This is not to say that we should not or cannot act until all people are free "from want and fear" (President Franklin Roosevelt's Four Freedoms Speech, 1941). It is to say that for very many, imagining "otherwise" and manifesting alternative lifeways will fail to take precedence in the face of the more pressing needs our subsistence and sensibilities depend on. Moving toward a global, sustainable inclusive community must prioritize freedom from want and fear for all, while carving out the intentional spaces that allow us to nurture and inspire otherwise possibilities. As a central crossroads where public discourse about who we are and how we want to live together (Hess & McAvoy, 2014) is negotiated, higher education has the potential to generate such spaces, to furnish the building grounds where collective understanding and alternative imaginaries can materialize. Colleges and universities represent the communal hubs where members of democratic society can engage diverse peoples and lifeways, and expand their worldview. They facilitate the indispensable collaborative encounters that enable humans to reconcile their experiences of the past and present, mediate their vision and hopes for the future, and aspire to an emboldened public imagination that embraces possibility.

Redesigning Design to Retrofit the Future

Education cannot save us; we have to save education.

—Bettina Love (2019)

For education to realize its transformative potential as implored by UNE-SCO and the opening chapter of this book—to move the needle on the cultural values, social structures, economic arrangements, and relational configurations around which climate change converge—we must question how our ability to even imagine alternative visions and lifeways might be constrained. How might education as we know it confine us within insular conceptualizations of "language, knowledge, agency, autonomy, identity, criticality, art, sexuality, earth, time, space, and self," in ways that foreclose "what is possible for us to sense, understand, articulate, want, and imagine?" (Stein et al., 2020, p. 58). Recognizing the limitations and inertia that higher education—or all education—place on our ability to imagine otherwise, scholars have suggested parallel spaces where freedom to experiment facilitate an expanded repertoire of possibilities.

Authors of the Sustainable Development Solutions Network (SDSN)[1] guide *Accelerating Education for the SDGs in Universities* recognize that the "deep and radical transformations" needed to achieve the 2030 Global Goals will require institutional change and a "Copernican turn in the way we approach every one of our activities" (Kestin et al., 2020, p. 38). Traditional approaches to education reform and organizational operations, prefaced on simple incrementalism, will not enable transformation at the depth, scale, and pace needed to address the problems facing us. Reinventing processes of change that build on "multi-stakeholder" cooperation, alternative plat-forms, and capacity to "upgrade our mental and social operating systems" must circumvent the structural barriers to innovation and collaboration permeating higher education (Scharmer, 2018a, as quoted in Kestin et al., 2020, p. 38). For tertiary education, the SDSN proposes parallel testing grounds, a "second operating system" where experimentation, innovation, and organizational reform avoids jeopardizing day-to-day operations and institutional survival of universities.

A 2.0 operating system would devote time and energy to developing alternate structures and mechanisms characterized by agility, creativity, and cross-fertilization that circumvent firmly cemented university hierarchies and governance. SDSN outlines some of the central characteristics that such a parallel operating system would include: community convened around shared purpose; new core functions of organization (integration, caring, facilitation, deep listening and conversation, curiosity, compassion, and courage); a "holding environment" for critical daily practices (hard conversations, accountability, information flow, etc.); self-management, wholeness, and evolutionary purpose; and more (Kestin et al., 2020, p. 39). The objective would be to influence how the university and academics function, and to implement structures and operations that refashion campuses as living laboratories of change and sustainability innovation. As ambitious and unrealistic as this may sound at this political moment—amid a collapsing neoliberal world order (Sitaraman, 2019)—proposals like this force us to envision the possibilities, to "freedom dream" (Garza, 2020; Kelley, 2022) beyond the "Cartesian dream" (Pereira & Funtowicz, 2015) and maintain a semblance of hope for a sustainable future.

Education must seek to do more than chip away at the edges in expanding otherwise possibilities; it must manifest throughout education and learning the will and wisdom to recast possibilities as expansive—infinite, adaptive, interactive, and forever evolving, intact with our sense of the times and reality or not. A cartography of social, sentient, or soft science sustainability—whatever best describes the transmogrifying competencies that guide our affective relations and sensibilities—is an incomplete heuristic device and visual aid designed to appreciate the complexity, inseparability, adaptability, and vitality at the core of a reality that is never fully in our control, that is far from perfect or "excellent," and that instead may be no more than ordinary, less than ordinary, or distinctively nonordinary, yet is more than good enough if we "stay with the trouble" *together* (Haraway, 2016). A social cartography of soft science sustainability is a playground for peer-to-peer (P2P) experimentation.

The concept of social cartography as a conduit for exploring the metacognitive, sentient, and psychosocial competencies upon which sustainability depends is essentially an invitation to enter into dialogue across difference of all kind; to add new, to rearrange, or to resist existing ingredient parts; to experiment with benchmarks, measures, templates, tutorials, lesson plans, rubrics, guides, activities, approaches, and frameworks that are forever tentative and preliminary, so that we may breathe life, courage, and kindness into the Global Goals and all the possible solutions—small or large—upon which the earth ultimately depends. Like pieces of a multidimensional jigsaw puzzle—the parts shapeshifting as we attempt to make sense of their meanings and configurations—this may require upending how we imagine problem-solving, innovation, and design altogether; it may require redesigning design. It will require that we be comfortable with the discomfort of unfamiliar and destabilizing imaginaries. Because imagining otherwise aims to disrupt the status quo, it demands critical self-reflection, cultural reflexivity, and historical reckoning, and threatens hegemonic power and political dislocation.

Otherwise imaginaries exist in contradistinction to existing, entrenched imaginaries that cast their long shadow on emergent possibilities by way of the past, entrusted upon the living like a nightmare (Marx, 1852). They summon struggles over painful, protracted histories only partially, if at all, included in mainstream national storylines and currently raging across much of the Western hemisphere as the fallout of colonialism comes home to roost and migration from the global South has intensified (Mayblin & Turner, 2021). Interrogating the intellectual, affective, and material economies of value upon which current-day modernity and coloniality build, Stein et al. (2020) question the potential for education to inspire *otherwise* imaginaries and modes of existing *together* in a world predominantly configured by domination and separability: "What educational processes can override modern socialized habits and embodied responses (fears, anxieties, self-interest, narratives, ego, narcissistic tendencies, wounds, etc.), to activate a sense of entanglement, responsibility, humility, and generosity . . . and open up possibilities/worlds that are viable, but unimaginable or inarticulable within our current frames of reference?" (p. 59).

In the majority of instances across the globe, envisioning and becoming "otherwise" will incite past and persistent harm and pain, beckoning reconciliation and repair before alternative possibilities can materialize. In the U.S., the oppression, disadvantages, and damages are profound,

> [including] 246 years of brutal enslavement; the rape of black women for the pleasure of white men and to produce more enslaved workers; the selling off of black children; the attempted genocide of Indigenous people, Indian removal acts, and reservations; indentured servitude, lynching, and mob violence; sharecropping; Chinese exclusion laws; Japanese American internment; Jim Crow laws of mandatory segregation; black codes; bans on black jury service; bans on voting; imprisoning people for unpaid work; medical sterilization and experimentation; employment discrimination; educational discrimination; inferior schools; biased laws and policing practices; redlining

and subprime mortgages; mass incarceration; racist media representations; cultural erasures, attacks, and mockery; and untold and perverted historical accounts. (Diangelo, 2018, p. 59)

Thus, central to the potential alternative sociopolitical, economic, and ecological modes of existence that otherwise imaginaries enable is human affect and ability to reconcile the past (Stein et al., 2020, p. 46). Stein et al. (2020) invoke the metaphor of "composting" to digest historic harm and to resist the reinventive thrust of "harmful habits of knowing, being, hoping and desiring" (Stein et el., 2020, p. 46). As subjects who have been socialized within systems, structures, and institutions of modern coloniality, intentional forays into countercolonial narratives and disaggregating the ways in which coloniality saturate our lives is essential. To "compost" is to work toward identifying, interrupting, and transforming destructive colonialities (past and present) into something different, generative, and creative, and to resist reproducing their underlying structures of harm (Stein et al., 2020, p. 54).

In their efforts to engage possibilities "otherwise," Stein et al. (2020) contrast the recursive colonial habits, desires and entitlements that we inherit—premised on material accumulation, consumption, and hierarchies of human value—with our want and longing for other ways of relating and existing. The persistent and far-reaching inequalities related to basic human rights and needs, justice, dignity, and belonging that COVID-19 and the Black Lives Matter movement brought to the fore dig deep into the alcoves of imperialism, nationalism, racism, sexism, and other forms of oppression. If we hope to negotiate alternatives, imaging *otherwise* and existing *together* demands that we expand our field of vision and collective imagination, and step outside circular logic that reproduce, reinforce, or reinvent power asymmetries, domination, violence, and inequity.

As a central theme in the storyline of modern colonial lifeways, race as a construct, and the atrocities that racism and shifting racialization inflict, remain profound for peoples around the world. Black feminist scholar Bettina Love (2019) explains "the conditions that preserve dark suffering . . . [as] the result of hundreds of years and multiple continents' commitment to creating and maintaining destructive, insidious, racist ideals that uphold White supremacy and anti-Blackness" (p. 22). Race, racialization, and racism can only be understood as the brutal underbelly of power and its dehumanizing but productive (extractive) biopolitics. As Mbembe (2002) demonstrates in "Necropolitics," its darkest realm remains where death and brutality, destitution and suffering are justified. Scholars conceptualize racism as a worldwide system of global apartheid, with firm roots in domination, violence, and oppression, designed to consolidate and maintain wealth and power (Besteman, 2019; Hage, 2017; Harrison, 2008; Mullings, 2008; Winant, 2008). For the Australian anthropologist Ghassan Hage (2017), the roots of racism are one and the same as those we can trace to ecology and all things living. In *Is Racism an Environmental Threat?*, Hage (2017) ferrets out the realities of overdetermined domestication—what he coins the "overdomination of generalized domestication"—as a mode of existence that builds on notions of Others as separate, and that negates mutualism and reciprocity.

To reclaim a mutualist mode of existence in which boundaries of all kinds between humans and other-than-humans recede or are broken down, so that we can experience interdependent reciprocity (Hage, 2017, p. 119), we must reign in "the exploitative will to power" and open up spaces where otherwise ways of "willing life" can emerge from the margins (p. 125). Although Hage (2017) recognizes domestication as an instinctive mode of existence and sustenance, he draws careful attention to the relational responsibilities of respect, mutuality, and indebtedness for the gifts we take from the earth but fail to honor and oblige in return. Such analyses resonate with the work of authors featured throughout chapters of this book, who understand all things living on earth as essentially intertwined. Premised on the notion of "interexistance," Hage's (2017) understanding of a mutualist mode of existence is anchored in entangled multiplicities that defy monorealism and monorelations. All social relations, he concludes, comprise entangled multiplicities, but because overdetermined practices of domestication and separability (have) delimit(ed) alternate possibilities and lifeways, the (mono)realities and (mono)relations grounded in racist and ecological destructive modes of domination have proliferated (Hage, 2017, p. 123).

For vast numbers of people today, and in the past, "overdomination of generalized domestication" implicates the biopolitics of power (Foucault, 2008), control over bodies, and careful management of life and lifeways, in ways that continue to be both insidious and ruthless. The residual traumas that endure from the violence these forms of domination, domestication, and separability (Othering) inflict have been the subject of investigations from various disciplinary perspectives. The role of historical and trans-generational trauma, for instance, has gained traction as a recognized source of social and individual suffering that deserves far greater attention.

Kirmayer et al. (2014) reference *historical trauma* as a construct used to describe the lasting effects of colonization and historical oppression on different Indigenous peoples in North America and elsewhere. The literature on historical and transgenerational trauma is multifaceted and complex, spanning vast cultural and religious diasporas and time frames, but a brief analysis of its significance for learning and unlearning, reconciling harm, and healing in order to move toward a sustainable common future follows.

Transgenerational Trauma and Collective Healing

The emergent prominence of historical and transgenerational trauma acknowledges the importance of reconciling harmful dislocations that histories of violence and oppression leave behind. The saliency of this expanding field and praxis resonate with education efforts underway to engage difficult and "courageous conversations" (Singleton & Linton, 2006), to teach historically and culturally responsive education (Muhammad, 2020), to link social-emotional learning (SEL) to cultural competency and culturally responsive practices (Simmons, 2019), and to do "more than survive" (Love, 2019). As McCarthy and Sealy-Ruiz (2010) explain, "a fear of the past can inhibit the freedoms of the present, as pedagogic practices that deny complex, and even contradictory, histories bind learners to normative narratives" (p. 75).

The stakes of history—of who tells the tale and how tales are told—are far from incidental or coincidental. How can we know who we are, McCarthy and Sealy-Ruiz ask, "if we do not know where we came from?" (2010, p. 75). This question is more poignant now than ever, with the assault on critical race theory (CRT) unfolding across the United States. At the time this was written, the CRT Forward Tracking Project (at the UCLA School of Law) reported 750 anti-CRT efforts introduced at various local, state, and federal levels nationwide. They were prompted in response to former president Donald Trump's Executive Order on Combating Race and Sex Stereotyping, EO 13950 (aka the Trump Truth Ban or Equity Gag Order), which sought to prohibit "divisive concepts" in teaching or training. Despite President Joe Biden's revocation of the order in 2021, governments at different levels (district, county, city, state) have joined in the offensive to prohibit learning about the history of race from critical perspectives. The fallout remains widespread and highly politicized, and is yet a painful reminder of how deeply embedded white supremacy is.

In deconstructing the narratives of planation life featured in Eric Williams's (1944) seminal *Capitalism and Slavery*, McCarthy and Sealy-Ruiz (2010) distinguish a "profound antipathy, a deep-bodied hostility towards the people's history" that cannot be mistaken for tacit or benign neglect (2010, p. 76). By and large, the knowledge, empathy, and compassion warranted in response to the enormous struggles and triumphs of oppressed people have been actively suppressed from normative accounts (McCarthy & Sealy-Ruiz, 2010). As the sites where formal education is institutionalized, schools and schooling become ground zero for organizing, producing, and reproducing mainstream knowledge, with sweeping capacity to impose upon impressionable minds. To explicitly suppress or avoid teaching "difficult history" (McCarthy & Sealy-Ruiz, 2010) in itself becomes a form of violence and trauma that denies, silences, erases, disempowers, distorts, or steals legacies, truth, traditions, and people's heritage.

Burgeoning interest in the field of transgenerational trauma includes comparative research on the impact that "genocide and other forms of massive, organized violence" have for differing groups of people across generations (Kirmayer et al., 2014). In "The Legacy of Trauma," DeAngelis (2019) references scholarship on the intergenerational effects of collective and historical trauma across cultural contexts, including the Holocaust, the Khmer Rouge killings in Cambodia, the Rwandan genocide, Native American genocide and displacement, and the enslavement of African Americans. The transmission of traumatic effects across generations has been studied over the longest period of time among Holocaust survivors and their offspring. More recently, research attention has expanded to the multigenerational impact and "shared stress" that slavery has inflicted in the United States (DeGruy, 2017; Williams et al., 2018).

Psychology scholars and clinical workers emphasize the importance of examining the intergenerational effects of trauma for understanding and addressing psychological and psychosocial suffering at its roots (Bombay et al., 2009; Gilda, 2014; Isobel et al., 2018; Menzies, 2010). Knowledge about the lasting consequences of collective trauma provides a gateway for developing healing interventions that do not evade historical harm people experience worldwide, but also for reclaiming and cultivating genius, for honoring suppressed or disqualified talent, aptitude, creativity, and brilliance (Love, 2019; Muhammad, 2020). Thus, the concept of transgenerational trauma should not be used to reduce people's experience or cultural identity to trauma, nor to pathologize cultural groups of people as sociohistorically inferior in any way (i.e., the culture of poverty). As

Ibram X. Kendi notes, traumatic and dehumanizing oppressions did not actually "succeed in dehumanizing Black people and leaving them adversely traumatized" and dysfunctional (2016, para. 3).

Theories that advance notions of Black people as degenerate or deficient, and that trace such inferiority to historical oppression—what Kendi terms the *oppression-inferiority thesis*—reinforce racist notions in the name of post-traumatic pathology. They harken back to recurring, false hypotheses that root " 'dysfunctional' Black behaviors in biology or culture" (Kendi, 2016, para. 7). Contrary to such depictions of dysfunction, the historical record in fact reveals great feats of cultural countenance, with Black people active in "politics, labor organizing, artistry, entrepreneurship, club building, church building, school building, community building—buildings that were oftentimes razed not by self-destructive PTSS [post-traumatic slave syndrome], but the fiery hand of Jim Crow" (Kendi, 2016, para. 12).

Activist Kimberly Jones's profound expression of outrage over critiques against the Black Lives Matter protests during the summer of 2020, demonstrates piercing legitimate despair over the debauchery that upholds white supremacy. Her powerful YouTube video comparing the game of Monopoly to the economic inequality that Black Americans experience deserves acclaim far beyond the popular reach of social media. It serves as a potent reminder of how important it is to understand the history and impact of deeply rooted social inequality. The video makes plain how the "social contract" conceived by erstwhile white, male Enlightenment thinkers (Hobbes, 1651; Locke, 1823; Rousseau, 1762) has yet to materialize in equal measure for many marginalized peoples. To say so with rightful ire and impeccable clarity is to send long overdue shockwaves through unsuspecting sheltered minds. A snippet follows:

> There's a social contract that we all have that . . . if you steal or if I steal, then the person who is the authority comes in and they fix the situation. But the person who fixes the situation is killing us. So the social contract is broken. . . . You broke the contract for 400 years. We played your game [of Monopoly] and built your wealth. You broke the contract when we built our wealth again [and again] on our own, by our bootstraps . . . when we built . . . Rosewood and you came in and you slaughtered us. You broke the contract. So fuck your Target, fuck your Hall of Fame. As far as I'm concerned they could burn this bitch

to the ground. And it still wouldn't be enough. And they are lucky that what Black people are looking for is equality and not revenge. (Jones, 2020)

The Black Lives Matter movement crystallized as an entrenched crisis of police brutality and criminal *in*justice, with penetrating roots in historic racialization and racism (Alexander, 2010), yet its deliberative thrust remains inseparable from injustices that prevail across sectors of society—including health, education, employment, housing, and so forth. Kirmayer et al. (2014) use the concept of transgenerational trauma to capture persistent patterns of inequity related to health and well-being among marginalized groups of people (Kirmayer et al., 2014). Their analysis importantly distinguishes transgenerational trauma from ongoing structural inequities and violence, acknowledging the need to address widening disparities in wealth and resources while disaggregating their historic genealogies.

Confronting historic atrocity is difficult, however. It requires "courageous conversations" (Singleton & Linton, 2006) and must prepare to bear the burden of trauma and pain with sensitivity, compassion, and care. Courageous conversations must be careful not to belabor or blame the "attitudes and behaviors" of oppressed groups—as the culprit that requires intervention, "civilizing," or resocializing under the euphemism of "healing" (Kendi, 2016, para. 15). The need for "civilizing" or "resocializing" remains at the hands of white supremacy, with all the liability that centuries of dehumanization and oppression against Other peoples have left behind. Ginwright (2018) affirms the value of trauma-informed approaches, but contends that they are often incomplete and can thus misconstrue understanding. Despite shedding important light on the particular needs of individuals exposed to trauma, current formulations of trauma-informed responses "presumes that . . . trauma is an individual experience, rather than a collective one" (Ginwright, 2018, para. 7). In other words, despite the need to address experiences of trauma, trauma-informed responses are not always adequately equipped to respond to their root causes at the collective level within communities, schools, or families (Ginwright, 2018).

Critics of the trauma-informed "deficit model"—with its continued focus on dysfunction among marginalized groups—are mindful of the power that language and terminology can have for creating blind spots, and prefer to centerstage healing rather than trauma itself. They caution against producing or reproducing reductive misrepresentation and erasure of human experience, no matter how good the intentions (Ginwright, 2018; Kendi, 2016). According to Ginwright, the designation "trauma-informed" foregrounds pathology rather than healing and restoration. The absence of pathology, the author notes, does not necessarily constitute well-being (Ginwright, 2018). These critiques, moreover, invoke the dangers of voyeurism, trauma porn and ethnic tourism, that place people's pain on display and that reduce humans to spectacle, curiosity, or commodity. In efforts to move toward perspectives that address and respect trauma across scope and scale—individual, collective, and intergenerational—we need holistic "healing-centered approaches" that address the roots and complexities of traumatic experience (Ginwright, 2018).

The power of language to represent, repress, or distort aside, trauma-informed pedagogies approach learning from the vantage point of compassion and understanding, and seek to recognize the impact that trauma and adverse childhood experiences (ACEs) can have for development and functioning—emotional, social, and cognitive (Dutil, 2020; Cavanaugh, 2016; Felitti et al., 1998). As a pedagogical approach, it refers to a set of principles that guide understanding about harm and its effects on people's mental, physical, and emotional health. Emphasis is placed on treating individuals as whole persons, rather than fixating on particular symptoms or behaviors (Ginwright, 2018). The Substance Abuse and Mental Health Services Administration (SAMHSA) identifies six principles of trauma-informed approaches: safety; trustworthiness; empowerment, collaboration, peer support; and history, gender, and culture (Dutil, 2020; SAMHSA, 2014).

There is growing evidence related to the last of these—history, gender, and culture—that experiences of racism and race-based stressors have adverse and cumulative effects for emotional health and well-being (Complex Trauma Treatment Network, 2016). Distress, trauma, and the development of PTSD is increasingly linked to racial bias, discrimination, and intergenerational transmission of trauma (Dutil, 2020). Scholars argue that in order to move toward comprehensive and representative approaches in education—that recognize, honor, and respond to all students and their right to matter and thrive (Love, 2019; Muhammad, 2020)—pedagogy must become responsive to the high rates of trauma that BIPOC students endure; it must infuse cultural and historical literacy, and critical race theory, in efforts to account for systemic racism prevalent throughout education (Dutil, 2020; McGee & Stovall, 2015).

Trauma-informed pedagogy aims to integrate into learning what Native American scholar Brave Heart and colleague DeBruyn (1998) define as "a legacy of chronic trauma and unresolved grief across generations" (p. 60). When denied or invisibilized as part of mainstream historical accounts, in particular, historical trauma can be passed along to subsequent generations (Brown-Rice, 2013). In the United States, for instance, the 1883 federal law that denied Native Americans the right to mourn their historic loss of life and land according to Indigenous tradition, compounded the enormous trauma inflicted upon them (Brown-Rice, 2013). Reconciling and restoring the harm and transgenerational effects that oppression of this magnitude has caused, and that centuries of denial have sought to repress, is the burden we bear. Culturally and historically responsive pedagogies connect learning and education to students' cultural-historical backgrounds and lived experiences in order to honor their perspectives and "support engagement, achievement, and empowerment" (Muñiz, 2020, p. 2), but are often difficult to engage.

Glenn Singleton's trademarked "courageous conversation" protocol provides a set of parameters for navigating contentious subject matter and classroom volatility. Prefaced on four agreements that guide dialogue, the model encourages students to expect and experience discomfort, to stay engaged, to speak their truth, and to accept non-closure. Defined as "authentic, sustained and compelling intra- and interracial dialogue to eradicate racism," courageous conversations comprise long overdue efforts to connect people across race and ethnicity in order to catalyze and bring about transformative social change (Courageous Conversations Global Foundation, n.d.). They are part and parcel of a long-past-due praxis that "stays with the trouble" (Haraway, 2016) in efforts to upend deep-seated habits of denial, suppression, and invisibility, and to unlock possibilities foreclosed.

We have much to learn from these, and other longstanding, horizontally structured (circle) approaches to intercultural exchange, conflict, and reconciliation. Healing-centered approaches, historically and culturally responsive pedagogies, and courageous conversations resonate with the tenets of diverse conciliatory praxis, including Indigenous practices, alternative dispute resolution (ADR) and conflict mediation, restorative circles (RC), intergroup dialogue,[2] and nonviolent communication (NVC),[3] alongside other peace initiatives referenced in chapter 3 (compassionate collaboration competency). None of these models present a panacea. Instead they prove the messy relevancy of inclusive, representative participatory processes—rather than end-goal alone—and recognize that determining the terms of debate and parameters that guide negotiations (rules of the game) must be part of the process. To expand on Kimberly Jones's metaphor of playing Monopoly according to rigged rules of hierarchy: Who establishes the playbook, and why are we playing Monopoly in the first place? Who decides which games we play and rules we follow?

These and similar critical questions animate the significance of language at a deeper level, beneath the words and terms we use, and encourage us to appreciate structures of meaning from the perspective of framing—what feminist philosopher Nancy Fraser describes as the "deep grammar of frame-setting in a globalizing world" (2005, p. 13). Despite phony varieties of diversity dialogue, intercultural exchange, and conflict negotiation—that remain largely cosmetic and perfunctory—experimentation with organic, unscripted exchange of ideas and divergent worldviews can expand our field of vision and view of what is possible. They broaden our opportunities to perceive alternate ways of seeing, thinking, being, and making sense of the world, based in reasoning that exists beyond the bounds of hidden bias and prescribed rationalities, including binary presumptions, simplistic adversarial jurisprudence, and zero-sum solutions.

Making real and actual a beloved community, a "diverse, equal and inclusive" (DEI) community, and a common sustainable future, means disrupting deeply engrained conceptualizations and configurations—partial and slanted in favor of a few, productive but potently destructive, and hurtful to humans and other-than-humans—in order to unearth the wealth of knowledge and possibilities that exist at the margins. It will require "creativity, imagination, boldness, ingenuity and a rebellious spirit—the methods that abolitionists demanded" (Muhammad et al., 2020, p. 421; Love, 2019). Borrowing from, building on, and beckoning the decolonizing and abolitionist teachings of freedom fighters, critical theorists of all kind, Black Feminists, Indigenous scholars and practitioners, postcolonial thinkers, and more, we need to welcome and nurture agitation literacy (Muhammad et al. 2020) above all, so that emerging students can open up and level the collective playing field.

Sentient Knowledge: Intelligence of the Heart

In *The Essentials of Theory U*, MIT scholar and public speaker Otto Scharmer (2018b) argues that "the most important tectonic shift of our lifetime is not behind but right in front of us" (p. 1). It includes "the transformation of capitalism, democracy, education and self" (Scharmer, 2018b,

p. 1). The historical moment we are living in, according to Scharmer, is one of "profound possibility and disruption," as marked by the "dying of an old mindset and logic of organizing" (Scharmer, 2018b, p. 3). Although what is emerging in its place is not exactly clear, Scharmer believes our consciousness is shifting from "ego-system to eco-system" (2018b, p. 3) in response to the state of "organized irresponsibility" in which we currently live (Scharmer, 2018b; Mills, 1956). In his chapter "The Blind Spot," Scharmer shares hopeful aspirations of awakening an awareness activated by the "intelligence of the heart" (2018b, p. 3).

Scharmer's theory of presence and learning from the emerging future, of allowing a new or different future to emerge (that "wants to come"), entails transcending the barriers of a tripart void or divide: ecological, social, and spiritual. The *ecological divide* is defined by unprecedented environmental destruction and loss of nature, and is represented by a single number: 1.5 (Scharmer, 2018b). We currently consume the resources of 1.5 planets, or 1.5 times what the earth can regenerate (Scharmer, 2018b). For the United States specifically, this number increases to 5, with the consumption rate exceeding more than what 5 planets can regenerate (Scharmer, 2018b). The *social divide* is defined by "obscene levels of inequity and fragmentation" and the loss of a collective society (Scharmer, 2018b, p. 5). This divide is summed up by the number 8: eight billionaires own more than the bottom half of the world's population. The *spiritual divide* is defined by the escalating levels of depression and burnout, and diminishing sense of fulfillment, and can be summed up by 800,000: the number of people who commit suicide every year (Scharmer, 2018b, p. 5).

Scharmer's "intelligence of the heart" elucidates the vitality of compassion and care as the lifeblood that will enable us to chart more sustainable futures together—compassion and care for the earth (ecological divide), for each other (social divide), and for ourselves (spiritual divide). All three divides are interconnected, but to transcend their triangulated ruptures, we must learn to live with each other and all life on earth with compassion and care. Intelligence of the heart is the "red thread" that runs through all soft science competencies needed to address climate change—criticality, collaboration, complexity. It is what ties us to each other and all things living, whether as soulmates or romantic partners (as in the East Asian red thread of fate), as a universal collective or commons that binds us all to each other, or as the prophetic symbolism evoked in Scandinavian lore: the through line and global theme that makes all else make sense.

Traced to the Greek myth of Theseus and the Minotaur, Nordic interpretations of the red thread are captured in the struggle to navigate a labyrinth (life) so complicated that no one could find their way out. Located deep within the labyrinth center was the darkest force (Minotaur, or environmental destruction) and threat, from which the city (earth) must be saved. That the workings of a maiden goddess (Ariadne) provides the (red) thread through which the pathway and protection is enabled is not incidental. In the matrilineal society of Minoan Crete, women are depicted as independent, with goddesses ruling absent male supervision. As the mighty leader of the labyrinth, the goddess on earth who represents fertility and weaving of life, Ariadne resonates with the autonomous and powerful women that so often characterize images of Viking life. What significance does the power of fertility and birth of life engender as the symbolic connective tissue that unites us through nurturance, protective care, and compassion? Its romantic, essentialist leanings aside, this question resounds with Arundhati Roy's (2003) visionary adage that "another world is not only possible, she's on her way. . . . On a quiet day, if I listen very carefully, I can hear her breathing" (p. 75). How do we still our minds and pause runaway time so that we can listen carefully to otherwise possibilities "on their way"?

Intelligence of the heart signifies the resolve of compassion and care in creating a beloved community that allows us to be wholly human and nonhuman, and that allows humans and other-than-humans to coexist and thrive together. It encourages the courage to be vulnerable, imperfect, and loved not in spite of our weaknesses but because of our weaknesses. Intelligence of the heart encourages us to disrupt tropes of excellence and perfection, so that we may "do more than survive" (Love, 2019) yet seek solace in good enough. It recognizes hierarchies of value—whether embedded in constructs of race, gender, sexuality, ability, intellect, or prowess—as false and damaging to our full potential. As Love (2019) argues, the goal is to "bring our full selves" and be "whole." When we do so, we breathe life into infinite possibilities.

Because so much of the global world and its social arrangements, systems, and institutions are deeply embedded in oppressive structures that need upending, we have a great deal to learn from those who have been actively resisting, interrupting, disrupting, subverting, surviving, and even thriving, in spite of the harm, hurt, distortion, denial, repression, and violence that white supremacy, racial capitalism, patriarchy, misogyny, and other forms of destruction wreak upon us. I am humbled by and indebted to antiracist, decolonizing, abolitionist, and feminist scholars, practitioners, advocates, and activists, particularly Black and Brown feminist thinkers, who against all systemic odds surmount—time and again—the struggle, pain, and grind of intersecting oppressions—acute, commonplace, and cumulative.

They rise against the tide of arrogant platitudes—about "resilience," demonstrating "grit," developing "character," espousing "moral" standards, displaying diligence in "work ethic," closing "achievement gaps," striving for "excellence"—despite knowing best themselves what to do, who they are, the strength that shapes them, how to raise their children, and how to distinguish right from wrong. They transcend insult added to injury while still able to love, build community, support each other, heal, and reach for our common humanity (Love, 2019). The spectacle of "education equity," with its tired diversity trainings and endless iterations of theatrical reform (i.e., No Child Left Behind, Race to the Top)—and its written statements, commitments, declarations, and disclaimers against injustice and discrimination—are so old and lackluster they have become offensive.

Education must find ways to transcend the chokehold of established epistemologies and ontologies, to centerstage knowledge and understanding pushed to the margins or beyond contrived realms of possibility. Because the legacies of global racism and racial capitalism (Leong, 2013; Robinson, 1983) have been "reinforced by years of living in a white supremacist world, [uncovering] a deep whiteness that may not be seen as such even by antiracist whites" will require hard work (Bonilla-Silva, 2015, p. 81; Wise, 2008; Hughey, 2012). Racism and other forms of oppression-domination hide in expected and unexpected places. It remains the courageous task of teachers and students alike to devote time to, discern, and unlearn its deep grammar, and to listen carefully to but not wait for or turn to Black and Brown people, or assume that they or other marginalized groups of people are at their disposal, ready and willing, to elucidate, demonstrate, divulge, and deliberate on their behalf. This is particularly noteworthy during a time when authoritarianism and racist fascism has been on the rise worldwide, and the retraumatizing effects of excavating white supremacist storylines become as real and raw as the ongoing police brutality, violence, and trauma unfolding before our eyes.

Learning from diverse historical and cultural experiences is more than the sum of its substantive parts or theoretical analysis. Historically and culturally responsive learning must allow students to engage in genuine exchange of perspectives that inevitably juxtapose conflicts of interest. Intergroup dialogue should not come at the cost of marginalized students, however, who may feel forced "into academic conversations about their nightmares" (Pegoda, 2020, p. 4). Pegoda (2020) explains that "students who are Asian, Arab, Black, Chinese, Latin American, Pilipino, or a racialized minority in any other way don't necessarily [want or] need to talk more about race. It's their everyday life" (p. 4). We must be mindful of "the fatigue that comes with not just living through . . . events but also feeling compelled to watch, talk about, and process those events all over again" (Anderson et al., 2019, p. 20). Backdoor approaches to "courageous conversations" (Singleton & Linton, 2006) should encourage students to share experiences on their own terms, and avoid entrapping students of color with the de facto burden of representing racial minorities.

Reconciling with the past must allow groups that have been oppressed to "reflect upon the accumulated concrete experiences of their own lives, the lives of others who share their situation, and even those who died long ago" (Marable, 2006, p. 36). Such a dialogue demands resocializing white Americans who are "still taught to believe that 'being white' means never having to say they are sorry" (Marable, 2006, p. 4). Education must prepare for and take stock of denial, distrust, fear, shame, culpability, and self-justification on the part of people in privileged positions, as they contemplate their complicity in systems of oppression, willingly and knowingly or not. As agents of social change, students in particular must be availed the time and support to dialogue, disentangle, and unlearn assumptions they have never had to question, to make sense of alterity and worldviews different from their own, and to cultivate awareness about their unconscious biases. Such contemplation, dialogue, and sense-making enable students to examine the broader meanings of democratic belonging and participation, and our responsibility to each other and the earth we inhabit.

I join fellow scholars who acknowledge that "as a society we have provided [few] template[s] for interaction across racial/ethnic groups and [that] such interaction cannot be taken for granted in the college environment" (Gurin et al., 2002). Education requires curricular scaffolding that assists faculty and students with managing the complexities and conflicts that arise as part of intercultural dialogue. Understanding the politics of exclusion and hierarchies of human value upon which social inequalities build requires engaging unpalatable and painful facets of a deeply entrenched domination paradigm. Despite the discomfort this may rouse, it encourages student awareness about their location within systems of social power (McIntosh, 2010), and represents a point of departure for contesting the "violence of silence."

Historically and culturally responsive education inspires generative dialogue and provides opportunities to revisit the stories we tell, or do not tell, about the past and present. It encourages us to uncover buried truths, despite the difficulties of deliberating painful particulars. In order to encourage the democratizing potential of historically and culturally responsive teaching, faculty and students need "supportive environments in which disequilibrium and experimentation can occur" (Gurin et al., 2002, p. 362), and in which students can explore feelings related to their lived experience. Feminist scholars propose "pedagogy of discomfort" (Boler, 1999) as a means to accommodate the affective dimensions that diversity experiences and discourse engenders. It is a pedagogy that recognizes emotional components of learning as emerging from social relations, from the shared learning that transpires between people, not as vestiges contained within individuals (Prebel, 2016). In sum, learning that seeks to engage, destabilize, or disrupt social norms, values, and hegemonic discourse must recognize emotion as integral and generative, but also *relational* (Prebel, 2016). Because the role of emotion in learning and discerning taken-for-granted worldviews is relationally constituted, pedagogy must facilitate authentic, embodied interactive learning opportunities.

Inclusive, generative learning and understanding, embedded in social relations and meaningful dialogue, necessitates the "intelligence of our heart": compassion, empathy, attentive listening, trust, and vulnerability. For many, however, such intelligence is a privilege that depends on peace of mind and the wherewithal that allows us to lower our guard, open our hearts, and activate compassion. It is often reserved for those who do not exist at the threshold of survival, with its threats of scarcity and state of insecurity. To be vulnerable requires trust and willingness to take risk, and hinges on the contingent stakes involved. Bezo and Maggi's (2015) study of the transgenerational impacts of the Holodomor—the genocide by mass starvation in Soviet Ukraine during the early 1930s—documents what research participants described as "living in 'survival mode'" (p. 87) with each generation learning from the previous one to not "trust others" or the world.

This speaks to the barriers that conditions of scarcity, survival, and threats to life—real or perceived—present, as part of the lasting impact that historic trauma imposes on generations. If we are to "do more than survive" (Love, 2019) or exist in survival mode, become whole, and "bring our full selves" (Love, 2019), we must attend to, make amends with, and attempt to end the dislocations of historic and persistent trauma against marginalized peoples around the world. In other words, contemporary politics of sustainability depend on turbulent struggles over inequity, oppression, and domination that span space and time, scope and scale (Nonini & Susser, 2020), and ingredient dimensions of domination (racism, sexism, heterosexism, classism, ableism, and other isms). As Hage (2017) and other scholars proclaim, the roots of racism and climate change ultimately flow from the same source: a paradigm that exists in symbiotic relation to oppression and domination. In the modern era, this is also known as the "house that modernity built" (Stein et al., 2019b).

In their UNESCO publication *Learning to Become* with *the World*, the Common Worlds Research Collective cautions that unless we pivot away from perpetuating "delusional human-centric and exceptionalist preoccupations . . . education [will] become part of the problem, not the solution" (Taylor et al., 2020, p. 3; Silova et al., 2018; Komatsu et al., 2020). Sustaining ourselves and all things living on planet earth are "one and the same thing" (Taylor et al., 2020, p. 3). As a result, any imaginary or future that continues "to separate humans off from the rest of the world . . . [will be] futile" (Taylor et al., 2020, p. 3). Cartesian dualism and binary thinking are so deeply ingrained as part of our reasoning, curricula, pedagogies, and psyche, however, that we generally fail to see the fallacy of separability and to identify as false the belief that we—as human beings—are separate from each other or "somehow separate from the world around us and can act upon it with impunity" (Taylor et al., 2020, p. 2; Taylor & Pacini-Ketchabaw, 2018). Because our failure to imagine otherwise is directly linked to education, Taylor et al. (2020) advocate fundamentally reconfiguring the role of formal learning and "schooling in order to radically reimagine and relearn our place and agency in the world" (p. 3).

We need to do more than step outside the box. We need to recognize that there is no box, or that the box is but one possible shape—square, rigid, closed, and sharp at four edges—amid many, if indeed shape is even the appropriate metaphor. We need to stop thinking in boxes, checking boxes, separating life and each other into boxes, and learn from *pluriversal* local knowledges, world cosmologies, and organic practices that exist beyond the myopic horizon of Western colonial ways of knowing, thinking, and being (Taylor et al., 2020, p. 5). This means putting into wider circulation, and further developing, pedagogical paradigms and curricular content that flesh out and map harmful habits of being. As the basis around which sustainability competencies and knowledge accumulation can materialize, this entails generative, collaborative experimentation and cobbling together repertoires of learning—some already in formation, others still in the making. It entails continually relearning and learning to be comfortable with perpetual relearning (Paul, 1993).

If we are to rehumanize, but also post-humanize, and pry open education so we "do more than survive"—so that earth and its ecosystems survive, and *all* humans, as well as other-than-humans "matter" and are able to bring their "whole selves" and thrive (Love, 2019)—we need to counter the cult of individuality and separability, and invest in each other and all things living. That investment cannot happen without compassion, empathy, love, listening, and building a collective "beloved community." It cannot happen without the intelligence of the heart. In the first and final analysis, we need each other to survive. We need to learn from each other and learn to love each other. We need to learn from other humans and other-than-humans, and learn to love other humans and other-than-humans. To return to the opening passages of this book, reversing climate change will depend on commitment and determination that traverse the local-global world and common goals around which all unite. The world is indeed our village, but it will take more than the village we know. It will take a global "beloved community" where everyone matters, feels like they belong, does more than survive, and is able to thrive.

Notes

Introduction

1. Countries must increase their Nationally Determined Contributions (NDCs) threefold to achieve the below 2°C goal, and fivefold to achieve the 1.5°C goal (United Nations Environment Programme, 2019, p. x).

2. United Nations Educational, Scientific and Cultural Organization.

3. For a descriptive overview of these sustainability competencies see Osman et al. (2017, pp. 8–10).

Chapter 1

1. Typically traced Rittel & Webber (1973), "wicked problems" are complex social problems with no clear or singular solution, many of which include thorny issues related to climate change. The term is further defined and discussed in chapter 4.

2. Perhaps most notably in Latin America.

3. The depth of knowledge referenced here is not to be confused with the psycho-affective educational practice that Andreotti (2021) has coined "depth education."

Chapter 2

1. The Illuminator is an art-activist collective based in New York City that stage projection-interventions in public spaces.

Chapter 3

1. Truth and reconciliation commissions are official bodies that aim to discern and reveal historic government wrongdoing and reconcile its lasting conflict.

Chapter 4

1. Hall (1977) characterized cultures according to the degree of nonverbal context used in communication, ranging from low to high.

2. A descriptive explanation for each of these is featured in Kønig et al. (2017).

3. For example, general systems theory, system dynamics, human system dynamics, and living system theory.

4. Depression increased by 18.4 percent between 2005 and 2015 worldwide.

5. Combined classes bring students from outside prison together with students in prison to study together.

Chapter 5

1. A global initiative for the United Nations.

2. Intergroup dialogue is a structured form of curricular pedagogy that allows students to explore controversial issues from diverse cultural perspectives through guided discussion.

3. As developed by Marshall Rosenberg.

Bibliography

Abdi, A. A., & Shultz, L. (2008). *Educating for human rights and global citizenship.* State University of New York Press.

Adler, N. (2003). Communication across cultural barriers. In J. Bolten & C. Ehrhardt (Eds.), *Interkurturelle kommunikation: Texte und übungen zum interkulturellen handeln* (pp. 247–276). Wissenschaft & Praxis.

Alexander, M. (2005). *Pedagogies of crossing: Meditations on feminism, sexual politics, memory, and the sacred.* Duke University Press.

Alexander, M. (2010). *The new Jim Crow: Mass incarceration in the age of color-blindness.* The New Press.

Allen, P., & Boulton, J. (2011). Complexity and limits to knowledge: The importance of uncertainty. In P. Allen, S. Maguire & B. McKelvey (Eds.), *The Sage Handbook of Complexity and Management* (pp. 164–181). Sage Publications.

Alvarez, M. (2021, February 22). Cornel West: "My ridiculous situation at Harvard." *The Chronicle of Higher Education.* https://www.chronicle.com/article/cornel-west-my-ridiculous-situation-at-harvard.

American Association of Colleges and Universities (n.d.). *Critical thinking VALUE rubric.* AAC&U VALUE Rubric Development Project. Retrieved August 27, 2023, from https://www.aacu.org/initiatives/value-initiative/value-rubrics/value-rubrics-critical-thinking.

American Association of Colleges and Universities (2018). *Global engagement and spaces of practice: Exploring global challenges across disciplinary boundaries.* https://www.aacu.org/conferences/global/2018.

Amsler, S., & Facer, K. (2017). Introduction to "Learning the future otherwise: Emerging approaches to critical anticipation in education." *Futures, 94,* 1–5.

Amsler, S., & Facer, K. (2017). Contesting anticipatory regimes in education: Exploring alternative educational orientations to the future. *Futures, 94,* 6–14.

Anderson, R., Saleem, F., & Huguley, J. (2019, October 28). Choosing to see the racial stress that afflicts our Black students. *Phi Delta Kappan, 101*(3), 20–25.

Andreotti, V. (2011a). *Actionable postcolonial theory in education.* Palgrave Macmillan.

Andreotti, V. (2011b). (Towards) decoloniality and diversality in global citizenship education. *Globalization, Societies and Education, 9*(3–4), 381–397.

Andreotti, V. (2015). Global citizenship otherwise: Pedagogical and theoretical insights. In A. Shultz & T. Pillay (Eds.), *Decolonizing global citizenship education* (pp. 221–230). Sense Publishers.

Andreotti, V. (2021). Depth education and the possibility of GCE otherwise. *Globalisation, Societies and Education, 19*(4), 496–509.

Andreotti, V., Stein, S., Ahenakew, C., & Hunt, D. (2015). Mapping interpretations of decolonization in the context of higher education. *Decolonization: Indigeneity, Education & Society, 4*(1), 21–40.

Andreotti, V., Stein, S., Pashby, K., & Nicolson, M. (2016). Social cartographies as performative devices in research on higher education. *Higher Education Research & Development, 35*(1), 84–99.

Anyon, J. (1980). Social class and the hidden curriculum of work. *The Journal of Education, 162*(1), 67–92.

Appelbaum. Y. (2018, October). Losing the democratic habit. *The Atlantic, 322*(3), 74–77.

Arum, R., & Roksa, J. (2011). *Academically adrift: Limited learning on college campuses.* University of Chicago Press.

Ash, S., & Clayton, P. (2009). Generating, deepening, and documenting learning: The power of critical reflection in applied learning. *Journal of Applied Learning in Higher Education, 1*, 25–48.

Ashkenas, R. (2010, August 24). Is your culture too nice? *Harvard Business Review.* Retrieved August 27, 2023, from https://hbr.org/2010/08/is-your-culture-too-nice

Baaz, M. E. (2005). *The paternalism of partnership: A postcolonial reading of identity in development aid.* Zed Books.

Bamber, P., Lewin, D., & White, M. (2018). (Dis-)Locating the transformative dimension of global citizenship education. *Journal of Curriculum Studies, 50*(2), 204–230.

Barlow, A. (2013). *The cult of individualism: A history of an enduring American myth.* Praeger.

Barter, D. (2009). *Restorative circles training.* John Jay College of Criminal Justice (CUNY), New York City, March 2009.

Barter, D. (2012). Walking toward conflict. *Tikkum, 27*(1), 21–70.

Bastidas, E., & Gonzales, C. (2009). Social cartography as a tool for conflict analysis and resolution: The experience of the Afro-Colombian communities of Robles. *Peace and Conflict Studies, 15*(2), 1–14.

Bauman, Z. (1998). *Globalization: The human consequences.* Blackwell Publishers.

Beckert, S. (2014, December 12). Slavery and capitalism. *The Chronicle of Higher Education.* Retrieved August 27, 2023, from https://www.chronicle.com/article/slavery-and-capitalism/.

Beckett, A. (2019, June 25). The new left economics: How a network of thinkers is transforming capitalism. *The Guardian*. Retrieved August 27, 2023, from https://www.theguardian.com/news/2019/jun/25/the-new-left-economics-how-a-network-of-thinkers-is-transforming-capitalism.

Beinhocker, E. (2007). *The origin of wealth*. Random House.

Bellah, R., Madsen, R., Sullivan, W., Swidler, A., & Tipton, S. (1985). *Habits of the heart: Individualism and commitment in American life*. University of California Press.

Bellah, R., Madsen, R., Sullivan, W., Swidler, A., & Tipton, S. (1991, July 12). The good society: Shaping the institutions that shape us. *Commonweal*, 425–429. Retrieved August 27, 2023, from https://www.commonwealmagazine.org/sites/default/files/imce/30047/Bellah%201991.pdf.

Bennett, J. (2017, June 24). On campus, failure is on the syllabus. *The New York Times*. Retrieved August 27, 2023, from https://www.nytimes.com/2017/06/24/fashion/fear-of-failure.html.

Besteman, C. (2019). Militarized global apartheid. *Current Anthropology*, *60*(19), S26–38.

Bezo, B., & Maggi, S. (2015). Living in "survival mode": Intergenerational transmission of trauma from the Holodomor genocide of 1932–1933 in Ukraine. *Social Science & Medicine*, *134*, 87–94.

Boler, M. (1999). *Feeling power: Emotions and education*. Routledge.

Bombay, A., Matheson, K., & Anisman, H. (2009, November). Intergenerational trauma: Convergence of multiple processes among First Nations peoples in Canada. *Journal of Aboriginal Health*, *5*(3), 6–47.

Bonilla-Silva E (2015). More than prejudice: Restatement, reflections, and new directions in critical race theory. *Sociology of Race and Ethnicity*, *1*(1), 73–87.

Boulding, K. (1950/1981). *A reconstruction of economics*. Wiley.

Bourdieu, P. (1977). *Outline of a theory of practice*. Cambridge University Press.

Boushey, H. (2019). *Unbound: How inequality constricts our economy and what we can do about it*. Harvard University Press.

Brave Heart, M. Y. H., & DeBruyn, L. M. (1998). The American Indian holocaust: Healing historical unresolved grief. *American Indian and Alaska Native Mental Health Research*, *8*(2), 60–82.

Brookfield, S. (2012). *Teaching for critical thinking: Tools and techniques to help students question their assumptions*. Jossey-Bass.

Brown, T., & Martin, R. (2015, September). Design for action. *Harvard Business Review*, 57–64.

Brown-Rice, K. (2013). Examining the theory of historical trauma among Native Americans. *The Professional Counselor*, *3*(3), 117–130.

Byrd, J. A. (2011). *The transit of empire: Indigenous critiques of colonialism*. University of Minnesota Press.

Camillus, J. (2008, May). Strategy as a wicked problem. *Harvard Business Review*, 1–9.

Castells, M. (2010). *The information age: Economy, society, culture: Vol. 3. End of millennium* (2nd ed.). Wiley.

Cavanaugh, B. (2016). Trauma-informed classrooms and schools. *Beyond Behavior*, 25(2), 41–46.

Checkland, P. (1981). *Systems thinking, systems practice*. Wiley.

Christie, N. (1977). Conflicts as Property. *The British Journal of Criminology*, 17(1), 1–15.

Collins, P. H. (1990). *Black feminist thought: Knowledge, consciousness and the politics of empowerment*. Routledge Classics.

Common Wealth (n.d.). *Our goal*. Retrieved August 27, 2023, from https://www.common-wealth.co.uk/about.

Complex Trauma Treatment Network (2016). *Complex trauma: In urban African-American children, youth, and families*. The National Center for Child Traumatic Stress, pp. 1–4.

Costanza, R., Graumlich, L. J., & Steffen W. (Eds.). (2007). *Sustainability or collapse? An integrated history and future of people on the earth*. MIT Press.

Courageous Conversations Global Foundations (n.d.). *About us*. Retrieved August 27, 2023, from https://ccglobalfoundation.org.

D'Alisa, G., Demaria, F., & Kallis, G. (2014). *Degrowth: A vocabulary for a new era*. Routledge.

Daly, H. (1991). *Steady-state economics* (2nd ed.). Island Press.

Daly, H. (1999). *Ecological economics and the ecology of economics*. Edward Elgar.

Dankel. D., Vaage, N., & Van der Sluijs, J. (2017). Post-normal science in practice. *Futures, 91*, 1–4.

Davidson, C. N. (2017). *The new education: How to revolutionize the university to prepare students for a world in flux*. Hachette.

Davidson, C. N. (2023, March 16). *Designing the new college classroom* [Paper presented]. The 14th Annual Interdisciplinary and Individualized Majors Program Network Conference: The Future of Individualized and Interdisciplinary Studies Programs, The CUNY Graduate Center, New York City.

DeAngelis, T. (2019). The legacy of trauma. *Monitor on Psychology, 50*(2), 36.

De Graaf, J., & Batker, D. K. (2011). *What's the economy for, anyway?: Why it's time to stop chasing growth and start pursuing happiness*. Bloomsbury Publishing USA.

DeGruy, J. (2017). *Post traumatic slave syndrome: America's legacy of enduring injury and healing*. Paul DeGruy Publications.

De Oliveira Andreotti, V., Stein, S., Pashby, K., & Nicolson, M. (2016). Social cartographies as performative devices in research on higher education. *Higher Education Research & Development, 35*(1), 84–99.

DeRoma, V., Martin, K., & Kessler, M. (2003). The relationship between tolerance for ambiguity and need for course structure. *Journal of Instructional Psychology, 30*(2), 104–110.

Diangelo, R. (2018). *White fragility: Why it's so hard for White people to talk about racism*. Beacon Press.

DiResta, R. (2018, July 3). The complexity of simply searching for medical advice. *Wired*. Retrieved August 27, 2023, from https://www.wired.com/story/the-complexity-of-simply-searching-for-medical-advice/.

Dunbar-Ortiz, R. (2008). The opposite of truth is forgetting: An interview with Roxanne Dunbar-Ortiz by Chris Dixon. *Upping the Anti*, 6, 47–58.

Dutil, S. (2020, July). Dismantling the school-to-prison pipeline: A trauma-informed, critical race perspective on school discipline. *Children & Schools, 42*(3), 171–178.

Duval, S., & Wicklund, R. (1972). *A theory of objective self-awareness*. Academic Press.

Eades, J. S. (2005). Anthropology, political economy and world-system theory. In J. G. Carrier (Ed.), *A handbook of economic anthropology* (pp. 26–40). Edward Elgar Publishing.

Ecochallenge (n.d.). *Iceberg model: Learn about the theory and practice of systems thinking*. Retrieved August 27, 2023, from https://ecochallenge.org/iceberg-model/.

Elder, L. (2010, September). *Richard W. Paul: A biographical sketch. Foundation for Critical Thinking*. Retrieved August 27, 2023, from https://www.criticalthinking.org/data/pages/37/ff640b6d016307b54cad91e5a9d4edfd4f18adb74215a.pdf.

Eriksen, T. H. (2016). *Overheating: An anthropology of accelerated change*. Pluto Press.

Eurich, T. (2018, January 4). What self-awareness really is (and how to cultivate it). *Harvard Business Review*. Retrieved August 27, 2023, from https://hbr.org/2018/01/what-self-awareness-really-is-and-how-to-cultivate-it.

Felitti, V. J., Anda, R. F., Nordenberg, D., Williamson, D. F., Spitz, A. M., Edwards, V., & Marks, J. S. (1998). Relationship of childhood abuse and household dysfunction to many of the leading causes of death in adults: The Adverse Childhood Experiences (ACE) Study. *American Journal of Preventive Medicine, 14*(4), 245–258.

Festinger, L. (1957). *A theory of cognitive dissonance*. Row, Peterson.

Fiske, S. J., Crate, S. A., Crumley, C. L., Galvin, K., Lazrus, H., Lucero, & Wilk, R. (2014). *Changing the atmosphere. Anthropology and climate change*. Final report of the AAA Global Climate Change Task Force. American Anthropological Association.

Fiske, S. J., Hubacek, K., Jorgensen, A., Li, J., McGovern, T., Rick, T., Schor, J., Solecki, W., York, R., & Zycherman, A. (2018). *Drivers and responses:*

Social science perspectives on climate change, part 2. USGCRP Social Science Coordinating Committee. https://www.globalchange.gov/content/social-science-perspectives-climate-change-workshop.

Foucault, M. (2008). *The birth of biopolitics: Lectures at the Collège de France, 1978–1979*. Palgrave Macmillan.

Fraser, N. (2005). Reframing Justice in a Globalizing World. *New Left Review, 36*, 1–19.

Freire, P. (2010). *Pedagogy of the oppressed* (30th anniversary ed.). Continuum.

Funtowicz, S., & Ravetz, J. (1993). Science for the post-normal age. *Futures, 25*(7), 739–755.

Garza, A. (2020). *The purpose of power: How we come together when we fall apart*. One World.

Gelatt, H. (1989). Positive uncertainty: A new decision-making framework for counseling. *Journal of Counseling Psychology, 36*(2), 252–256.

Georgescu-Roegen, N. (1971). *The entropy law and the economic process*. Harvard University Press.

Gessen, M. (2016, December 13). The Putin paradigm: To what extent can Putin provide insight into Trump's understanding of power? *The New York Review of Books*. Retrieved August 27, 2023, from https://www.nybooks.com/online/2016/12/13/putin-paradigm-how-trump-will-rule/.

Gilda, G. (2014). The intergenerational trauma of slavery and its aftermath. *The Journal of Psychohistory, 41*(3), 181–197.

Gilmore, R. W. (2022). *Abolition geography: Essays towards liberation*. Verso.

Ginsberg, B. (2011). *The fall of the faculty: The rise of the all-administrative university and why it matters*. Oxford University Press.

Ginwright, S. (2018, May 31). *From trauma informed care to healing centered engagement*. Medium.

Giroux, H., & Purpel, D. (1983). *The hidden curriculum and moral education: Deception or discovery?* McCutchan Publishing.

Gorostiaga, J. (2017). Perspectivism and social cartography: Contributions to comparative education. *Educação & Realidade, 42*(3), 877–898.

Granovetter, M. (1985). Economic action and social structure: The problem of embeddedness. *American Journal of Sociology, 91*(3), 481–510.

Grenier, S., Barrette, A., & Ladouceur, R. (2005). Intolerance of uncertainty and intolerance of ambiguity: Similarities and differences. *Personality and Individual Differences, 39*(3), 593–600.

Grohs, J., Kirk, G., Soledad, M., & Knight, D. (2018). Assessing systems thinking: A tool to measure complex reasoning through ill-structured problems. *Thinking Skills and Creativity, 28*, 110–130.

Gunderson, L., & Holling, C. (2002). *Panarchy: Understanding transformations in human and natural systems*. Island Press.

Gunderson, L., Holling, C., & Light, S. (1995). *Barriers and bridges to the renewal of ecosystems and institutions*. Columbia University Press.

Gund Institute for Environment (n.d.). *Ecological economics*. Retrieved August 27, 2023, from https://www.uvm.edu/gund/ecological-economics.

Gurin, P., Dey, E., & Hurtado, S. (2002). Diversity and higher education: Theory and impact on educational outcomes. *Harvard Educational Review, 72*(3), 330–366.

Hage, G. (2017). *Is racism an environmental threat?* Polity Press.

Halberstam, J. (2011). *The queer art of failure*. Duke University Press.

Hall, E. (1977). *Beyond culture*. Anchor Books.

Hannerz, U. (1992). *Cultural complexity: Studies in the social organization of meaning*. Columbia University Press.

Haraway, D. J. (2016). *Staying with the trouble: Making kin in the Chthulucene*. Duke University Press.

Hari, J. (2022). *Stolen focus: Why you can't pay attention and how to think deeply again*. Crown Publishing.

Harley, J. (1988). Maps, knowledge, and power. In D. Cosgrove & S. Daniels (Eds.), *The iconography of landscape: Essays on the symbolic representation, design and use of past environments* (pp. 52–81). Cambridge University Press.

Harley, J. (2001). Deconstructing the map. In J. Harley & P. Laxton (Eds.), *The new nature of maps: Essays in the history of cartography* (pp. 150–168). John Hopkins University Press.

Harrison F. (2008). Global apartheid, foreign policy, and human rights. In M. Marable & V. Agard-Jones (Eds.), *Transnational Blackness: Navigating the global color line* (pp. 19–40). Palgrave Macmillan.

Harvey, D. (1990). *The condition of postmodernity: An enquiry into the origins of cultural change*. Blackwell.

Harvey, D. (2004). The "new" imperialism: Accumulation by dispossession. *Socialist Register, 40*, 63–87.

Harvey, D. (2005). *A brief history of neoliberalism*. Oxford University Press.

Heffernan, M. (2015). *Beyond measure: The big impact of small changes*. Simon & Schuster.

Held, D. (2000). Regulating globalization? The reinvention of politics. *International Sociology, 15*(2), 394–408.

Hess, D., & McAvoy, P. (2015). *The political classroom: Evidence and ethics in democratic education*. Routledge.

Hobbes, T. (1651/2010). *Leviathan: Or the Matter, Forme, and Power of a Commonwealth Ecclesiasticall and Civill* (Ian Shapiro, Ed.). Yale University Press.

Hoffman, D. (2015, July 1). Describing transformative civic learning and democratic engagement practices. *American Democracy Project*. Retrieved August 27, 2023, from https://adpaascu.wordpress.com/2015/07/01/describing-transformative-civic-learning-and-democratic-engagement-practices/.

Hoffman, J. (2020, August 13). Young adults report rising levels of anxiety and depression in pandemic. *The New York Times*. Retrieved August 27, 2023, from https://www.nytimes.com/2020/08/13/health/Covid-mental-health-anxiety.html.

Holling, C. (1978). *Adaptive environmental assessment and management.* John Wiley & Sons.

Horkheimer, M. (1982). *Critical theory.* Seabury Press.

Horowitz, D. (2011). *Philosophy in prison* [Video]. TED. https://www.ted.com/talks/damon_horowitz_philosophy_in_prison.

Hughey, M. (2012). *White bound: Nationalists, antiracists, and the shared meanings of race.* Stanford University Press.

Hung, W. (2008). Enhancing systems-thinking skills with modelling. *British Journal of Educational Technology, 39*(6), 1099–1120.

Ignatiev, N., & Garvey, J. (1996). *Race traitor.* Routledge.

Institute for the Study of Science, Technology and Innovation (n.d.). The University of Edinburgh. Retrieved August 27, 2023, from https://www.sps.ed.ac.uk/subject-area/science-technology-and-innovation-studies/about.

Isobel, S., Goodyear, M., Furness, T., & Foster, K. (2018). Preventing intergenerational trauma transmission: A critical interpretive synthesis. *Journal of Clinical Nursing, 28*(7–8), 1100–1113.

Johnson, W. (2013). *River of dark dreams: Slavery and empire in the cotton kingdom.* Harvard University Press.

Johnstone, G., & Van Ness, D. (Eds.). (2013). *Handbook of restorative justice.* Routledge.

Jonassen, D. H. (2000). Toward a design theory of problem solving. *Educational Technology Research and Development, 48*(4), 63–85.

Jones, K. (2020). *How can we win?* [Video]. YouTube. https://www.youtube.com/watch?v=llci8MVh8J4.

Kakutani, M. (2018, July 14). The death of truth: How we gave up on facts and ended up with Trump. *The Guardian.* Retrieved August 27, 2023, from https://www.theguardian.com/books/2018/jul/14/the-death-of-truth-how-we-gave-up-on-facts-and-ended-up-with-trump.

Kallis, G. (2018). *Degrowth.* Agenda Publisher.

Kaufman, B. (1999). *Power-dialogues: The ultimate system for personal change.* Epic Century Publishers.

Kelley, R. (2022). *Freedom dreams: The Black radical imagination.* Penguin Random House.

Kendi, I. X. (2016, June 21). Post-traumatic slave syndrome is a racist idea. *Black Perspectives.* Retrieved August 27, 2023, from https://www.aaihs.org/post-traumatic-slave-syndrome-is-a-racist-idea/.

Kestin, T., Lumbreras, J., & Puch, M. C. (2020). *Accelerating education for the SDGs in universities: A guide for universities, colleges, and tertiary and higher education institutions.* Sustainable Development Solutions Network.

https://irp-cdn.multiscreensite.com/be6d1d56/files/uploaded/accelerating-education-for-the-sdgs-in-unis-web_zZuYLaoZRHK1L77zAd4n.pdf.

Khoo, S., & Jørgensen, N. (2021). Intersections and collaborative potentials between global citizenship education and education for sustainable development. *Globalisation, Societies and Education, 19*(4), 470–481.

Kimmerer, R. W. (2013). *Braiding sweetgrass: Indigenous wisdom, scientific knowledge and the teachings of plants*. Milkweed Editions.

The King Center (n.d.). *The King Philosophy—Nonviolence 365*. Retrieved August 27, 2023, from https://thekingcenter.org/about-tkc/the-king-philosophy/.

Kirmayer, L., Gone, J., & Moses, J. (2014). Rethinking historical trauma. *Transcultural Psychiatry, 51*(3), 299–319.

Kitchin, R., Gleeson, J., & Dodge, M. (2013). Unfolding mapping practices: A new epistemology for cartography. *Transactions of the Institute of British Geographers, 38*(3), 480–496.

Kittler, M., Rygl, D., & Mackinnon, A. (2011). Beyond culture or beyond control? Reviewing the use of Hall's high-/low-context concept. *International Journal of Cross Cultural Management, 11*(1), 63–82.

Knight, F. (1921). *Risk, uncertainty and profit*. Houghton Mifflin.

Kolko, J. (2015). Design thinking comes of age. *Harvard Business Review, 93*(9), 66–71.

Komatsu, H., Rappleye, J., & Silova, I. (2020). Will education post-2015 move us toward environmental sustainability? In A. Wulff (Ed.), *Grading goal four* (pp. 297–321). Brill Sense.

Kønig, N., Børsen, T., & Emmeche, C. (2017). The ethos of post-normal science. *Futures, 91*, 12–24.

Krugman, P. (2020, July 27). The cult of selfishness is killing America: The right has made irresponsible behavior a key principle. *The New York Times*. https://www.nytimes.com/2020/07/27/opinion/us-republicans-coronavirus.html.

Kwai, I., & Peltier, E. (2021, February 14). "What's the point?" Young people's despair deepens as Covid-19 crisis drags on. *The New York Times*. Retrieved August 27, 2023, from https://www.nytimes.com/2021/02/14/world/europe/youth-mental-health-covid.html.

Lakoff, G. (2010). Why it matters how we frame the environment. *Environmental Communication, 4*(1), 70–81.

Lanham, R. (2006). *The economics of attention: Style and substance in the age of information*. University of Chicago Press.

LeBlanc, P. (2018, May–August). Higher education in a VUCA world. *Change: The Magazine of Higher Education*, 23–26.

Le Heron, R., & Lewis, N. (2007). Globalizing economic geographies in the context of globalizing higher education. *Journal of Geography in Higher Education, 31*(1), 5–12.

Leicht, A., Heiss, J., & Byun, W. (Eds.). (2018). *Issues and Trends in Education for Sustainable Development*. United Nations Educational, Scientific, and Cultural Organization (UNESCO). Retrieved August 27, 2023, from https://unesdoc.unesco.org/ark:/48223/pf0000261954.

Leong, N. (2013). Racial Capitalism. *Harvard Law Review, 126*(8), 2151–2226.

Levin, S. (1999). *Fragile dominion*. Perseus Books.

Lewen, J. (2012, April 8). *Learning and trust on the road to college readiness at San Quentin* [Video]. Big Ideas Fest, YouTube. http://www.youtube.com/watch?v=82nvE0BC2CA.

Liboiron, M. (2021). *Pollution is colonialism*. Duke University Press.

Liedtka, J. (2015). Perspective: Linking design thinking with innovation outcomes through cognitive bias reduction. *Journal of Product Innovation Management, 32*(6), 925–938.

Locke, J. (1823/2013). *The works of John Locke* (Vol. 1). Facsimile Publisher.

Lorde, A. (1984). *Sister outsider: Essays and speeches*. Crossing Press.

Love, B. (2019). *We want to do more than survive: Teaching and the pursuit of educational freedom*. Beacon Press.

Luft, J., & Ingham, H. (1955). The Johari window, a graphic model of interpersonal awareness. University of California, Los Angeles. *Proceedings of the Western Training Laboratory in Group Development*. Retrieved August 27, 2023, from https://emilms.fema.gov/is_0240c/groups/63.html.

Lyubansky, M., & Barter, D. (2011). A restorative approach to interpersonal racial conflict. *Peace Review: A Journal of Social Justice, 23*(1), 37–44.

Mallon, D. (2013, October 9). Restorative justice practice in tribal courts. *Wabanaki Legal News*. Retrieved August 27, 2023, from https://ptla.org/wabanaki/restorative-justice-practices-tribal-courts.

Marable, M. (2006). *Living Black history*. Basic Civitas Books.

Marx, K. (1994). *The eighteenth Brumaire of Louis Bonaparte*. International Publishers.

Mayblin, l., & Turner, J. (2021). *Migration studies and colonialism*. Polity.

Mbembe, A. (2002). Necropolitics. *Public Culture, 15*(1), 11–40.

McCarthy, C., & Sealy-Ruiz, Y. (2010). Teaching difficult history: Eric Williams' *Capitalism and Slavery* and the challenge of critical pedagogy in the contemporary classroom. *Power and Education, 2*(1), 75–84.

McEvoy, K. (2007). Beyond legalism: Toward a thicker understanding of transitional justice. *Journal of Law and Society, 34*(4), 411–440.

McGee, E., & Stovall, D. (2015). Reimagining critical race theory in education: Mental health, healing, and the pathway to liberatory praxis. *Educational Theory, 65*(5), 491–511.

McIntosh, P. (2010). *White privilege: Unpacking the invisible knapsack*. Seed: Seeking Educational Equity and Diversity. Wellesley Centers for Women, Wellesley College.

McKibben, B. (2010). *Eaarth: Making a life on a tough new planet*. Times Books.

McNeill, N., Douglas, E., Koro-Ljungberg, M., Therriault, D., & Krause, I. (2016). Undergraduate students' beliefs about engineering problem solving. *Journal of Engineering Education, 105*(4), 560–584.

Menkel-Meadow, C. (2007). Restorative justice: What is it and does it work? *Annual Review of Law and Social Science, 3*, 161–187.

Menzies, P. (2010). Intergenerational trauma from a mental health perspective. *Native Social Work Journal, 7*, 63–85.

Metcalfe, J. (2007). Alfred Marshall and the general theory of evolutionary economics. *History of Economic Ideas, 15*(1), 81–110.

Mika, C. (2019). Confronted by Indigenous metaphysics in the academy: Educating against the Tide. *Beijing International Review of Education, 1*(1), 109–122.

Miller, C., Groth, O., & Mahon, J. (2018). Management innovation in a VUCA world: Challenges and recommendations. *California Management Review, 61*(1), 5–14.

Mills, C. W. (1945). The powerless people: The social role of the intellectual. *Bulletin of the American Association of University Professors, 31*(2), 231–243.

Mills, C. W. (1956/2000). *The power elite*. Oxford University Press.

Mills, N. (2012, Fall). The corporatization of higher education. *Dissent*. https://www.dissentmagazine.org/article/the-corporatization-of-higher-education

Miranda, C. (2020, October 30). U.S. individualism isn't rugged, it's toxic—and it's killing us. *L.A. Times Entertainment and Arts*. Retrieved August 27, 2023, from https://www.latimes.com/entertainment-arts/story/2020-10-30/how-toxic-individuality-is-tearing-the-u-s-apart.

Mirowski, P. (1991). *More heat than light. Economics as social physics, physics as nature's economics*. Cambridge University Press.

Mirowski, P. (2013). *Never let a serious crisis go to waste: How neoliberalism survived the financial meltdown*. Verso Books.

Mitchell, S. (2009). *Unsimple truths: Science, complexity, and policy*. University of Chicago Press.

Mogel, L., & Bhagat, A. (2007). *An atlas of radical cartography*. Journal of Aesthetics and Protest.

Moore, E., & Garzón, C. (2010, Fall). Social cartography: The art of using maps to build community power. *Race, Poverty & the Environment*, 66–67. Retrieved August 27, 2023, from https://www.reimaginerpe.org/files/Moore.Garzon.17-2.pdf.

Muhammad, G. (2020). *Cultivating genius: An equity framework for culturally and historically responsive literacy*. Lois Bridges.

Muhammad, G., Dunmeyer, A., Starks, F., & Sealey-Ruiz, Y. (2020). Historical voices for contemporary times: Learning from Black women educational theorists to redesign teaching and teacher education. *Theory into Practice, 59*(4), 419–428.

Mullings, L. (2008). Race and globalization. In M. Marable & V. Agard-Jones (Eds.), *Transnational Blackness: Navigating the global color line* (pp. 11–18). Palgrave Macmillan.

Muñiz, J. (2020). Culturally responsive teaching: A reflection guide. *New America*. https://www.newamerica.org/education-policy/policy-papers/culturally-responsive-teaching-competencies/.

Naess, A. (1973). The shallow and the deep, long-range ecology movement: A summary. *Inquiry, 16*(1–4), 95–100.

Nair, S. (2017). Postcolonialism. In S. McGlinchey, R. Walters & C. Scheinpflug (Eds.), *International relations theory*. E-International Relations Publishing.

Narayan, K. (1993). How native is a "native" anthropologist? *American Anthropologist, 95*(3), 671–686.

National Academy of Sciences (2004). *Facilitating interdisciplinary research. Committee on Science, Engineering, and Public Policy*. National Academy Press.

National Task Force on Civic Learning and Democratic Engagement (2012). *A crucible moment: College learning & democracy's future*. Association of American Colleges & Universities. Retrieved August 27, 2023, from https://www.aacu.org/publication/a-crucible-moment-college-learning-democracys-future.

Nelson, R., & Winter, S. (1982). *An evolutionary theory of economic change*. Harvard University Press.

Nocella, A. (2011). An overview of the history and theory of transformative justice. *Peace & Conflict Review, 6*(1), 1–10.

Noguera, P. (2003). The trouble with Black boys: The role and influence of environmental and cultural factors on the academic performance of African American males. *Urban Education, 38*(4), 431–459.

Nonini, D., & Susser, I. (Eds.). (2020). *The tumultuous politics of scale: Unsettled states, migrants, movements in flux*. Routledge.

Osman, A., Ladhani, S., Findlater, E., & McKay, V. (2017). *A curriculum framework for the sustainable development goals*. Commonwealth Secretariat. Retrieved August 27, 2023, from https://www.thecommonwealth-ilibrary.org/index.php/comsec/catalog/book/1064.

Pais, A., & Costa, M. (2020). An ideology critique of global citizenship education. *Critical Studies in Education, 61*(1), 1–16.

Papenfuss, J., Merritt, E., Manuel-Navarrete, D., Cloutier, S., & Eckard, B. (2019). Interacting pedagogies: A review and framework for sustainability education. *Journal of Sustainability Education, 20*. Retrieved August 27, 2023, from http://www.susted.com/wordpress/wp-content/uploads/2019/04/Papenfuss-JSE-April-2019-General-Issue-PDF-3.pdf.

Pashby, K., Costa, M., Stein, S. & Andreotti, V. (2021). Mobilising global citizenship education for alternative futures in challenging times: An introduction. *Globalization, Societies and Education, 19*(4), 371–378.

Patel, L. (2014). Countering coloniality in educational research: From ownership to answerability. *Educational Studies, 50*, 357–377.

Patil, L., Dutta, D., & Bement, A., Jr. (2015). *Educate to innovate. Factors that influence innovation: Based on input from innovators and stakeholders.* National Academies Press.

Paul, R. (1993). *Critical thinking: How to prepare students for a rapidly changing world.* Foundation for Critical Thinking.

Paulston, R. (1994). Comparative education: Paradigms and theories. In T. Husen & N. Postlethwaite (Eds.), *International encyclopedia of education* (pp. 923–933). Pergamon Press.

Paulston, R. (Ed.). (1996). *Social cartography: Mapping ways of seeing social and educational change.* Garland Science.

Paulston, R., & Liebman, M. (1994). An invitation to postmodern social cartography. *Comparative Education Review, 38*(2), 215–232.

Pegoda, A. (2020, August 12). Suggestions for teaching about race. *Inside Higher Ed.* https://www.insidehighered.com/advice/2020/08/12/advice-teaching-about-race-and-racism-class-fall-opinion.

Pellmar, T., & Eisenberg, L. (2000). Barriers to interdisciplinary research and training. In T. C. Pellmar & L. Eisenberg (Eds.), *Bridging disciplines in the brain, behavioral, and clinical sciences* (pp. 41–57). National Academy Press.

Pereira, Â., & Funtowicz, S. (Eds.). (2015). *Science, philosophy and sustainability: The end of the Cartesian dream.* Routledge.

Pereira, Â., & Saltelli, A. (2017). Post-normal institutional identities: Quality assurance, reflexivity and ethos of care. *Futures, 91*, 53–61.

Polanyi, K. (1944). *The great transformation: The political and economic origins of our time.* Farrar & Rinehart.

Prebel, J. (2016, Summer). Engaging a "pedagogy of discomfort": Emotion as critical inquiry in community based writing courses. *Composition Forum, 34.* http://compositionforum.com/issue/34/

Pynchon, T. (1973). *Gravity's rainbow.* Penguin Press.

Ravetz, J. R. (1987). Usable knowledge, usable ignorance: Incomplete science with policy implications. *Knowledge, 9*(1), 87–116.

Raworth, K. (2017). *Doughnut economics: Seven ways to think like a 21st century economist.* Chelsea Green Publishing.

Rayner, S. (2012). Uncomfortable knowledge: The social construction of ignorance in science and environmental policy discourses. *Economy and Society, 41*(1), 107–125.

Reidmiller, D., Avery, C., Easterling, D., Kunkel, K., Lewis, K., Maycock, T., & Stewart B. (2018). *Fourth National Climate Assessment: Vol. 2. Impacts, Risks, and Adaptation in the United States.* U.S. Global Change Research Program. https://doi.org/10.7930/NCA4.2018.RiB.

Reyer, C., Bachinger, J., Bloch, R., Hattermann, F., Ibisch, P. L., Kreft, S., Lasch, P., Lucht, W., Nowicki, C., Spathelf, P., Stock, M., & Welp, M. (2012). Climate change adaptation and sustainable regional development: A case study for the Federal State of Brandenburg, Germany. *Regional Environmental Change*, *12*, 523–542.

Rittel, H., & Webber, M. (1973). Dilemmas in a general theory of planning. *Policy Sciences*, *4*(2), 155–169.

Ritterman, J. (2017, January 19). *The beloved community: Martin Luther King Jr.'s prescription for a health society*. HuffPost. Retrieved August 27, 2023, from https://www.huffpost.com/entry/the-beloved-community-dr_b_4583249.

Robinson, C. (1983). *Black Marxism: The making of the Black radical tradition*. Pluto Press.

Rockström, J., Steffen, W., Noone, K., Persson, Å., Chapin III, F. S., Lambin, E. F., Lenton, T. M., Scheffer, M., Folke, C., Schellnhuber, H. J., Nykvist, B., de Wit, C. A., Hughes, T., van der Leeuw, S., Rpdje, H., Sörlin, S., Snyder, P. K., Costanza, R., Svedin, U., . . . Foley, J. A. (2009). A safe operating space for humanity. *Nature*, *461*, 472–475.

Rodriguez, D. (2018). Abolition as praxis of human being: A foreword. *Harvard Law Review*, *132*, 1575.

Rosa, E., & Dietz, T. (2012). Human drivers of national greenhouse gas emissions. *Nature Climate Change*, *2*, 581–586.

Rosenberg, M. (2003). *Nonviolent communication: A language of life* (2nd ed.). PuddleDancer Press.

Rousseau, J. (1762/1968). *The social contract*. Penguin Books.

Rowe, A. C., & Tuck, E. (2016, June 20). Settler colonialism and cultural studies: Ongoing Settlement, cultural production, and resistance. *Cultural Studies ↔ Critical Methodologies*, *17*(1), 3–13.

Roy, A. (2003). *War talk*. South End Press.

Ruitenberg, C. (2007). Here be dragons: Exploring cartography in educational theory and research. *Complicity: An International Journal of Complexity and Education*, *4*(1), 7–24.

Sachs, J. (2015). *End of poverty: Economic possibilities for our time*. Penguin Books.

Sahlins, M. (2009). Hunter-gatherers: Insights from a golden affluent age. *Pacific Ecologist*, *18*, 3–8.

Salazar, J. (2015, June 23). Buen Vivir: South America's rethinking of the future we want. *The Conversation*. Retrieved August 27, 2023, from https://theconversation.com/buen-vivir-south-americas-rethinking-of-the-future-we-want-44507.

Scharmer, O. (2018a, January 8). *Education is the kindling of a flame: How to reinvent the 21st-century university*. HuffPost. Retrieved August 27, 2023, from https://www.huffpost.com/entry/education-is-the-kindling-of-a-flame-how-to-reinvent_b_5a4ffec5e4b0ee59d41c0a9f.

Scharmer, O. (2018b). *The essentials of theory U: Core principles and applications*. Berrett Koehler Publishers.

Schick, A., Hobson, P., & Ibisch, P. (2017). Conservation and sustainable development in a VUCA world: The need for a systemic and ecosystem-based approach. *Ecosystem Health and Sustainability*, 3(4), 1–12.

Schön, D. A., & Rein, M. (1994). *Frame reflection: Toward the resolution of intractable policy controversies*. Basic Books.

Selibas, D. (2021, February 8). *Buen Vivir: Colombia's philosophy for good living*. BBC Travel. Retrieved August 27, 2023, from https://www.bbc.com/travel/article/20210207-buen-vivir-colombias-philosophy-for-good-living.

Sen, S. (n.d.). *It takes a child to raise a village*. UNESCO Mahatma Gandhi Institute of Education for Peace and Sustainable Development. Retrieved August 27, 2023, from https://mgiep.unesco.org/article/it-takes-a-child-to-raise-a-village.

Seppälä, E. (2013, June 3). Compassion: Our first instinct. *Psychology Today*. Retrieved August 27, 2023, from https://www.psychologytoday.com/us/blog/feeling-it/201306/compassion-our-first-instinct.

Seppi, J. (1996). Spatial analysis in social cartography: Metaphors for process and form in comparative educational studies. In R. Paulston (Ed.), *Social cartography: Mapping ways of seeing social and educational change* (pp. 121–139). Garland.

Sessions, G. (Ed.). (1995). *Deep ecology for the twenty-first century*. Shambhala.

Sessions, G. (2014). Deep ecology, new conservation, and the anthropocene worldview. *The Trumpeter*, 30(2), 106–114.

Shiva, V. (1998). The greening of global reach. In G. Thuatail, S. Dalby & P. Routledge (Eds.), *The geopolitics reader* (pp. 230–143). Routledge.

Shotwell, A. (2016). *Against purity: Living ethically in compromised times*. University of Minnesota Press.

Shultz, L. (2007). Educating for global citizenship: Conflicting agendas and understandings. *Alberta Journal of Educational Research*, 53(3), 248–258.

Silova, I., Komatsu, H., & Rappleye, J. (2018). Facing the climate change catastrophe: Education as solution or cause? *Worlds of Education*. https://www.norrag.org/facing-the-climate-changecatastrophe-education-as-solution-or-cause-by-iveta-silova-hikaru-komatsu-and-jeremy-rappleye/.

Silva, D. F. D. (2014). Toward a Black feminist poethics: The quest(ion) of blackness toward the end of the world. *The Black Scholar*, 44(2), 81–97.

Simmons, D. (2019). You can't be emotionally intelligent without being culturally responsive: Why family and consumer sciences must employ both to meet the needs of our nation. *Journal of Family & Consumer Sciences*, 111(2), 7–16.

Simon, H. (1955). A behavioral model of rational choice. *The Quarterly Journal of Economics*, 69(1), 99–118.

Singer, B. (2007). The U.S. oil fix. In L. Mogel & A. Bhagat (Eds.), *An atlas of radical cartography*. Journal of Aesthetics and Protest Press.

Singleton, G., & Linton, C. (2006). *A field guide for achieving equity in schools: Courageous conversations about race*. Corwin.

Sitaraman, G. (2019). *The great democracy: How to fix our politics, unrig the economy, & unite America*. Basic Books.

Smith, N. (2004). *American empire: Roosevelt's geographer and the prelude to globalization*. University of California Press.

Standing, G. (2016). *The precariat: The new dangerous class*. Bloomsbury Academic.

Stein, S. (2016, October 26). *Facing up to the colonial present of U.S. higher education*. Medium. Retrieved August 27, 2023, from https://medium.com/@educationotherwise/facing-up-to-the-colonial-present-of-u-s-higher-education-62f6a16428ec.

Stein, S. (2017, December 5). *So you want to decolonize higher education? Necessary conversations for non-Indigenous people*. Medium. Retrieved August 27, 2023, from https://medium.com/@educationotherwise/https-medium-com-educationotherwise-so-you-want-to-decolonize-higher-education-4a7370d64955.

Stein, S. (2018a). Beyond higher education as we know it: Gesturing towards decolonial horizons of possibility. *Studies in Philosophy and Education, 38*, 143–161.

Stein, S. (2018b, Autumn). Rethinking critical approaches to global and development education. *Policy & Practice: A Development Education Review, 27*, 1–13.

Stein, S. (2019a). The ethical and ecological limits of sustainability: A decolonial approach to climate change in higher education. *Australian Journal of Environmental Education, 35*(3), 198–212.

Stein, S. (2019b). Navigating different theories of change for higher education in volatile times. *Educational Studies, 55*(6), 667–688.

Stein, S., Andreotti, V., Suša, R., Amsler, S., Hunt, D., Cash, A., Elwood, J., Čajková, T., Valley, W., Cardoso, C., Siwek, D., Pitaguary, B., Pataxó, U., D'Emilia, D., Calhoun, B., & Okano, H. (2020). Gesturing towards decolonial futures: Reflections on our learnings thus far. *Nordic Journal of Comparative International Education, 4*(1), 43–65.

Stroh, D. (2015). *Systems thinking for social change: A practical guide to solving complex problems, avoiding unintended consequences, and achieving lasting results*. Chelsea Green Publishing.

Substance Abuse and Mental Health Services Administration [SAMHSA] (2014). *SAMHSA concept of trauma and guidance for a trauma-informed approach*. https://store.samhsa.gov/product/SAMHSA-s-Concept-of-Trauma-and-Guidance-for-a-Trauma-Informed-Approach/SMA14-4884.

Suša, R., & de Oliveira Andreotti, V. (2019). Social cartography in educational research. In G. Nobilt (Ed.), *Oxford Research Encyclopedia of Education*.

Tallon, R. A., & McGregor, A. (2014). Pitying the Third World: Towards more progressive emotional responses to development education in schools. *Third World Quarterly, 35*(8), 1406–1422.

Tauritz, R. (2012). How to handle knowledge uncertainty: Learning and teaching in times of accelerating change. In A. Wals & P. Corcoran (Eds.), *Learning for sustainability in times of accelerating change* (pp. 299–315). Wageningen Academic Publishers.

Taylor, A., & Pacini-Ketchabaw, V. (2018.) *The common worlds of children and animals: Relational ethics for entangled lives.* Routledge.

Taylor, A., Silova, I., Pacini-Ketchabaw, V., & Blaise, M. (2020). *Learning to become with the world: Education for future survival.* Common Worlds Research Collective. United Nations Educational, Scientific and Cultural Organization (UNESCO). Retrieved August 27, 2023, from https://unesdoc.unesco.org/ark:/48223/pf0000374032.

Thunberg, G. (2021, July 1). *Austrian World Summit address* [Video]. YouTube. https://www.youtube.com/watch?v=YNL43SaOur0.

de Tocqueville, A. (2000). *Democracy in America.* (H. Mansfield & D. Winthrop, Eds.). Chicago University Press.

Tuck, E., & Yang, K. W. (2012). Decolonization is not a metaphor. *Decolonization: Indigeneity, Education & Society, 1*(1). https://jps.library.utoronto.ca/index.php/des/article/view/18630.

Tugend, A. (2020). *On the verge of burnout: Covid-19's impact on faculty well-being and career plans.* The Chronicle of Higher Education Report.

United Nations (2019). *Global Sustainable Development Report 2019: The Future is Now—Science for Achieving Sustainable Development.* Secretary-General Independent Group of Scientists. https://reliefweb.int/report/world/global-sustainable-development-report-2019-future-now-science-achieving-sustainable.

United Nations Department of Economic and Social Affairs (2020). *United Nations Sustainable Development Goals Report 2020.* United Nations Publications. https://unstats.un.org/sdgs/report/2020/The-Sustainable-Development-Goals-Report-2020.pdf.

United Nations Environment Programme (2019, November 26). *Emissions Gap Report 2019.* https://www.unep.org/resources/emissions-gap-report-2019.

Usarralde, M. (2006). La educación comparada revisitada: Revisión a la evolución epistemológica y temática en la era postcomparada. *Tendencias Pedagógicas, 11,* 77–102.

Van Asselt, M. (2000). *Perspectives on uncertainty and risk: The prima approach to decision support.* Kluwer Academic Publishers.

Visser, J., & Visser, Y. (2004). Ambiguity, cognition, learning, teaching, and design. *TechTrends, 48*(1), 40–43.

Walker, J., Taneja, A., Abuel-Ealeh, S., & Pearce, C. (2016). *Private profit, public loss: Why the push for low-fee private schools is throwing quality education off track*. The Right to Education Initiative. https://campaignforeducation.org/en/2016/06/29/private-profit-public-loss/.

Wallerstein, E. (2004). *World systems analysis: An introduction*. Duke University Press.

Walters, C. (1986). *Adaptive management of renewable resources*. Macmillan.

Weber, M. (1949). *Max Weber on the methodology of the social sciences*. (E. Shils & H. Finch, Trans.). Free Press.

Welch, A. (1993). Class, culture and the state in comparative education: Problems, perspectives and prospects. *Comparative Education, 29*, 7–27.

Williams, E. (1944). *Capitalism and slavery*. University of North Carolina Press.

Williams, M., Printz, D., & DeLapp, R. (2018). Assessing racial trauma with the Trauma Symptoms of Discrimination Scale. *Psychology of Violence, 8*(6), 735–747.

Willinsky, J. (1998). *Learning to divide the world: Education at empire's end*. University of Minnesota Press.

Wilson, C. (2014). *Performance coaching: A complete guide to best practice coaching and training*. Kogan Page.

Winant, H. (2008). The modern world racial system. In M. Marable & V. Agard-Jones (Eds.), *Transnational Blackness: Navigating the global color line* (pp. 41–53). Palgrave Macmillan.

Wise, T. (2008). *White like me: Reflections on race from a privileged son*. Soft Skull Press.

World Health Organization (2017). *Depression and other common mental disorders: Global health estimates*. https://apps.who.int/iris/bitstream/handle/10665/254610/WHO-MSD-MER-2017.2-eng.pdf.

The World We Want (2013). *Breaking down the Silos: Integrating environmental sustainability in the post-2015 agenda*. Retrieved August 27, 2023, from https://www.undp.org/publications/breaking-down-silos-integrating-environmental-sustainability-post-2015-agenda.

Xepapadeas, A. (2016). Ecological economics. In S. Durlauf & L. Blume (Eds.), *The New Palgrave Dictionary of Economics* (pp. 599–600). Palgrave Macmillan.

Young, O. (2006). Vertical interplay among scale-dependent environmental and resource regimes. *Ecology and Society, 11*(1), 1–16.

Young, O. R., Berkhout, F., Gallopin, G. C., Janssen, M. A., Ostrom, E., and van der Leeuw, S. (2006). The globalization of socio-ecological systems: An agenda for scientific research. *Global Environmental Change, 16*, 304–316.

Zraick, K. (2019, February 20). Teenagers say depression and anxiety are major issues among their peers. *The New York Times*. Retrieved August 27, 2023, from https://www.nytimes.com/2019/02/20/health/teenage-depression-statistics.html.

Index

science to address, 92; students, teaching to manage, 99–101, 104–106

Webber, M., 84, 135n1 (chap. 1)
What's the Economy for Anyway? (de Graaf and Batker), 25
"White Privilege: Unpacking the Invisible Knapsack" (McIntosh), 102
white supremacy, 55, 119, 121, 123, 124, 130
"wicked problems": about, 84–85, 135n1 (chap. 1); collaboration to address, 66, 75, 79; complexity of, 27; post-normal science to address, 93–94; strategy as, 84
Wicklund, R., 35
Williams, Eric, 122
Wilson, Carol, 78
women: economics, increased role in, 47–48; prisoners, 114–115. *See also* gender
World Summit on climate change (Austria, 2021), 1–2

Yang, K. W., 23, 69

Milton Keynes UK
Ingram Content Group UK Ltd.
UKHW041137020924
447770UK00007B/592